Academic Success Through Empowering Students

D1502989

Academic Success Through Empowering Students

by Cathy Vatterott

Foreword by J. Howard Johnston

NATIONAL MIDDLE SCHOOL ASSOCIATION
Columbus, Ohio

LB 1623.5
.V35
1999

NMSA

National Middle School Association
4151 Executive Parkway
Suite 300
Westerville, Ohio 43081
Telephone (800) 528-NMSA

Sue Swaim, Executive Director
Jeff Ward, Associate Executive Director
John Lounsbury, Senior Editor, Professional Publications
Edward Brazee, Associate Editor, Professional Publications
Mary Mitchell, Copy Editor/Designer
Marcia Meade, Senior Publications Representative
Andrea Yost, Cover Design

Library of Congress Cataloging-in-Publication Data
Vatterott, Cathy, date
    Academic success through empowering students/by Cathy Vatterott.
       p. cm.
    Includes bibliographical references (p.)
    ISBN 1-56090-160-8 (pbk.)
    1. Middle school students--United States. 2. Student participation in administration--United States. 3. Student participation in curriculum planning--United States. 4. Classroom environment--United States. 5. Academic achievement--United States.
I. Title
LB1623.5.V35   1999
373.236--dc21   99-22816
                                            CIP

To Dr. Bernie Epstein, Principal, Pattonville Heights Middle School, who for 30 years has inspired students and teachers to strive for excellence. Bernie personifies the heart and soul of middle level education.

About the Author

Dr. Cathy Vatterott is an associate professor of middle level education at The University of Missouri-St. Louis. A former junior high school teacher and middle school assistant principal, she frequently presents at national and state conferences and serves as a consultant to middle schools. This year she has been deeply humbled by the experience of being a middle school parent.

Acknowledgements

My special thanks:

...to the many middle school students, teachers, and administrators I have visited and worked with who have shared their ideas so unselfishly. This book would not be possible without their contributions.

...to the students, faculty, administrators, and support staff of Pattonville Heights Middle School, Maryland Heights, Missouri (especially those from 1984-1986), who first showed me the middle school philosophy in action and who continue to serve as one of the best examples of an exemplary middle school.

...to dedicated special education teachers who empower our most reluctant students every day through attitudes, techniques, and adaptations that serve as models for empowering all students.

...to J. Howard Johnston and Paul George, whose philosophies helped to shape my ideas and who always found time to provide resources, advice, and mentorship.

...to James Beane, whose writings and presentations profoundly changed my views about curriculum.

...to Alfie Kohn, whose writings and presentations brought clarity and validity to my ideas, and who so often expressed what I wanted to say so much better than I could. — C.V.

Contents

Foreword

Middle level educators are confronted with a daunting set of challenges and demands, not the least of which is to engage the attention and assure the academic success of students who are often preoccupied with matters ranging from normal adolescent transition issues to the more lethal aspects of life on the cusp of the millenium. As social issues and challenges have ballooned in more and more communities in the last decades of the 20th century, they have edged aside purely developmental or academic considerations of what makes an effective middle level school. These challenges are both pernicious and persistent:

- Despite a growing economy, more children live in poverty than at anytime since the Depression.

- There is a growing disparity between the school performance of poor, minority children and their more affluent counterparts on virtually all measures of school achievement.

- Teenage pregnancy, drug abuse, and criminal activity continue to be intractable problems among those children with the fewest educational, social, and emotional resources to cope with them.

- Student apathy, misbehavior, and overt challenges to adult and school authority are on the rise, and more adults see adolescents and their schools as chaotic and disorderly.

These social issues challenge the schools at the same time that public confidence in education is eroding. More states are establishing standards for academic performance and attaching promotion and graduation decisions to high-stakes testing programs. Local communities insist upon greater rigor in the schools' programs, placing more demands on already sorely taxed teachers and administrators. Large-scale movements in the states and local districts to create special alternatives for specific groups of students, ranging from gifted to delinquent, threaten to erode already scarce resources. Accountability has shifted to a focus on individual schools and, in some states, individual teachers, fueling a growing tendency to "teach only toward the test." Alternative and charter schools are springing up throughout North America, and the fastest growing student population is comprised of home-schooled children, their numbers now rivaling the enrollment of the Los Angeles public school system.

This is no time for tinkering. Public expectations are high. Parents and policy-makers are impatient. Alternatives exist and are promoted with sophisticated marketing and public relations strategies. Middle level educators are challenged on every front to redesign themselves and their schools to promote high levels of achievement in a developmentally appropriate setting that assures success for all learners. Indeed, the most effective schools of the opening decades of the new century will be those that adopt a "whatever it takes" stance to assure that every child meets high standards of academic performance, receives support in his or her growth through the potentially treacherous adolescent years, and is equipped to overcome unfair and unequal conditions of life to be successful citizens in a democratic society. It's a tall order, one that will require a clear vision and hard work.

In this volume, Cathy Vatterott sets out both a vision and a clear agenda for schools willing to carefully examine their most cherished practices in order to succeed with all children in the new century. She challenges us to commit to a just, fair, and rigorous curriculum for all learners and to support all children as they confront demanding but engaging authentic learning tasks.

Dr. Vatterott refreshes our view of the links between development and learning, paying particular attention to the kinds of human relations and emotional skills necessary for success in the new collaborative environments of effective middle level schools. She argues convincingly for giving students a powerful voice in these new learning communities – empowering them to be full participants in decisions that affect their lives, including the ones that have always been reserved for adults, namely curriculum and instruction. Only in this manner can we expect our youth to be prepared for the collaborative, democratic, information-driven, loosely coupled organizations that define contemporary life.

For those old enough to remember the turbulent 60s and 70s, Dr. Vatterott's proposal to fully empower students is mildly unsettling; but her careful reasoning and articulate vision of schools where children succeed and learn through collaborative work with adults and one another is both reassuring and compelling. She examines thoroughly the concept of power and how it is productively applied in cooperative, interdependent settings. She explores with care and sensitivity the impediments to sharing power in schools and offers clear, reasonable, and convincing suggestions for practitioners.

This is, first and foremost, a sympathetic and affirming book for practitioners. The author's deep roots in the schools are evident in the material she presents and the message she brings to teachers and school leaders. Dr. Vatterott's activist-scholar stance is clear throughout the work: she is writing to make things work better for more children. She not only argues for meaningful change, she actually shows us how to begin to do the hard work in our own schools and communities. She presents her plans clearly and with great sensitivity to the enormous challenges that teachers and administrators face every minute of every day. The rich resources included in the book convince us that we are not alone in this endeavor. We are encouraged to explore the initiatives, successes and frustrations of other schools and districts that are struggling to redesign themselves for the coming century, and we are provided with the resources and contacts to do so. Indeed, this is an empowering work for all teachers and administrators laboring at school reform and renewal. It helps us to believe, and rightly so, that we can meet the awesome challenges presented to us by a demanding public.

The stakes have never been higher for our children or their schools. Dr. Vatterott calls on all of us to be the best that we can be, secure in the knowledge that we can and will work hard to make a difference for all children. Her work enlightens us, challenges us, and guides us. A committed constructivist, she offers no simple solutions or formulas for success, insisting that each school and each professional wrestle individually with the issues and circumstances in their own communities in order to do "whatever it takes" for their children. Just as she says about learning, school reform and renewal is "messy and time consuming," but, with the guidance offered in this work, it seems somehow less daunting.

— J. Howard Johnston
University of South Florida, Tampa

I

The Philosophy of Empowerment
─────────────────────

I n 1968, *Wild in the Streets* was one of many films of that era deal-ing with the theme of social revolution. Now viewed as a cult classic (and categorized on video shelves as science fiction), the film professed the evils of a younger generation intent on removing everyone over the age of 30 from positions of power. In one crucial scene a father gives his teenage son an order which the boy refuses by saying, "I have the vote now, remember?" As the issue of empowering 14-year-old students is presented to teachers today, a similar scenario may come to mind.

In the turbulent '60s, the plot of *Wild in the Streets* played on the older generation's worst nightmare: everyone over age 30 confined to internment camps, neutralized with hallucinogenic drugs, and deprived of all power by a radical younger generation. In 1999, the idea of giving students power may seem just as frightening and radical to some middle level teachers and principals who feel today's youth already have ex-cess power.

Yet like the 1960s, these are turbulent times. In the 1990s, the fall of communism and the unification of Europe moved countries and gov-ernments toward egalitarian goals. In this country, democracy has evolved slowly. Women and blacks fought hard for and won the right to vote. This achievement was the inevitable result of the evolution of democracy, which continues to profoundly affect traditional power re-lationships in this country (Dreikurs, 1987). Children, once viewed as powerless, are gaining legal rights and protections once reserved only for adults. Reflecting the society at large, educators have struggled to reform their own antiquated power structures through building-based management, total quality management, collaborative decision mak-ing, teacher empowerment, and establishing learning communities. All of these were inevitable in the evolution of democratic schools. All these practices share a common element: teachers, administrators, and parents are working together in a collaborative fashion to improve schools.

Administrators work collaboratively with their customers – teachers. Gone are the vestiges of "scientific management" popularized early in this century by Frederick Winslow Taylor, whose watchwords were *compliance, control,* and *command*. This system was founded on fear, intimidation, and an adversarial approach to problem solving. Today it is in our best interest to encourage everyone's potential by dedicating ourselves to the continual improvement of our own abilities and those of the people with whom we work and live (Bonstingl, 1992).

As collaborative practices transform schools, the dimensions of the change will permeate all aspects of school life: the structure and organization of the school, curriculum and instruction, teaching and learning, and student and teacher assessment. Changes in teacher and administrator roles will impact the relationship between student and teacher.

> *Today it is in our best interest to encourage everyone's potential by dedicating ourselves to the continual improvement of our own abilities and those of the people with whom we work and live .*

How will the relationship between middle level teachers and students be altered? What is the middle level student's role in a collaborative school? It seems ludicrous to many enlightened educators today to suggest that teachers be excluded from decision making in schools. Yet, in many discussions about collaboration, students are not included. Even in middle schools that empower teachers, students are routinely excluded from participating in decisions or solving school problems that affect them. Skeptics would say that middle school students cannot be trusted to make decisions about their learning and are not mature enough or knowledgeable enough to be involved in decisions about school programs. Yet, "in a democratic school it is true that all of those directly involved in the school, including young people, have the right to participate in the process of decision making" (Apple & Beane, 1995, p. 9). Middle level students, at a social and moral crossroad, are uniquely poised to benefit from empowerment. Just as teacher empowerment can lead to improved motivation and productivity, student empowerment in middle level schools can produce equally valuable results.

An elite group of middle level students is already empowered in our present "star system" (Van Hoose & Strahan, 1988). Armed academically with literate parents, safe and comfortable homes, and few if any learning problems, these students have developed the skills and attitudes that enable them to be successful in school. With those skills and attitudes they have amassed a history of school success and learning-related self-esteem.

On the other hand, unsuccessful students in the middle school are at the bottom of the power hierarchy. They are disempowered, somehow not a part of the group. Politically speaking, they are oppressed. Coupled with a lack of control over the myriad changes of puberty, many of them react with apathy, withdrawal, hostility, or rebellion and earn the label of "at-risk" students.

Brain-based research has shown us that attitude is critical in the motivation to learn. Emotion drives attention, which drives learning and memory (Sylwester, 1995), and the perception of emotional threat causes learners to "downshift" and withdraw from the learning experience (Pool, 1997). A major factor contributing to a lack of motivation in students at risk is the disempowering nature of the school experience itself:

> Ability groups, grade retention, working alone, denial of strengths and focus on weaknesses, learning that is information-rich and experience-poor, and an irrelevant curriculum are all conditions that students must endure or ignore. Clearly the conditions educators have created are a major source of the problem rather than merely the helpless victims of cultural circumstances. (Barth, 1990, p. 126)

Empowering all students

True student empowerment means developing those skills and attitudes necessary for academic success in *all* students. Academic success is the central value of empowerment. Critical in the philosophy of student empowerment is the belief that empowerment will enable all students to succeed. Teachers must believe that all students deserve to be empowered, can be trusted to be empowered, and are capable of success (Rogers & Freiberg, 1994). The discrepancy between empowerment as commonly conceived in educational circles and the broader concept of power in our culture causes difficulties. Kreisberg (1992) defined empowerment as "a process through which people and/or communities increase their control or mastery of their own lives and the decisions that affect their lives" (p. 19). This definition reflects the commonly held view of teacher empowerment (Barth 1990).

Student empowerment could be defined similarly as a process by which students increase their control or mastery of their own learning and decisions that affect their classroom and school. This concept of empowerment appears inconsistent with how most people view power; indeed, the pervasive conceptions of power in our culture and emerging definitions and descriptions of empowerment seem to be in conflict. Predominant theories of power define it in terms of the ability to control others, to impose one's will on others. Power is viewed in terms of relationships of domination. This is the concept of power as "power over" (Kreisberg, 1992).

In an autocratic culture, power has traditionally been thought of simplistically as "power over." In this context, power exists in a limited quantity and people are either powerful or powerless. It is suggested that a balance of power exists, as on two sides of a scale, implying that as one person or group gains power another loses it. Conceptualized in this fashion, power relinquished is power lost, advantage lost. Any form of student empowerment would automatically result in teacher disempowerment. Add to this the unimpressive history of humanistic innovations in education (i.e., the open classroom, values clarification curriculum of the 70s, experiments in unbridled student freedom), and no wonder educators are uneasy about giving students power.

"Empowerment is a theory in search of a compatible conception of power" (Kreisberg, 1992, p. 22). Kreisberg suggests that the evolution of democracy in governments and social structures has created the need for a new concept of power.

> The definition of power as domination and control is limited; it is incomplete. There is another dimension, or form, or experience of power that is distinctly different from pervasive conceptions. The ignored dimension is characterized by *collaboration, sharing,* and *mutuality.* We can call this alternative concept 'power with' to distinguish it from 'power over.' (p. 61)

Collaborative schools reflect a view of power as "power with." For instance, if teachers and administrators work together to make decisions about curriculum, administrators are not exercising power over the teachers (in that decision) but are sharing "power with" them. Current strategies of quality circles and total quality management have employed the "power with" concept in the business world resulting in increased productivity and improved morale. The empowerment of teachers has shown similar advantages (Barth, 1990).

How does the "power with" concept apply to the empowerment of students? The essence of empowerment is trust, trust in the energy, commitment, imagination, and potential of teachers and principals (Barth, 1990). It is trust in the student's capacity to develop (Rogers, 1969), trust in people to "do the right thing," trust that is modeled daily by all adults within the school – secretaries, janitors, counselors, bus drivers, and teachers.

> *The essence of empowerment is trust:*
> *in the energy, commitment, imagination,*
> *and potential of teachers and principals.*

Beliefs about students and their relationships

The philosophy of empowering students is reflected in a series of beliefs about the nature of students and their relationship to teachers:

1. The ability to learn is influenced more by personal factors than by innate ability. School climate, interpersonal relationships, social and emotional needs, internal and external messages that students receive affect learning much more profoundly than presumed innate ability.

2. Children are inherently good, industrious, curious, and eager to learn. Optimism by teachers breeds success (George, Stevenson, Thomason, & Beane, 1992).

3. Learning is a naturally pleasant and intrinsically rewarding activity. It can, however, be made distasteful by sterile methods, lack of relevance, punitive grading systems, and lack of student input (Kohn, 1993).

4. All students can be successful learners but may require different paces or different paths (Slavin, 1997).

5. All progress in learning is valuable and motivating. Lack of progress is demotivating.

6. Student input is valuable and has worth. Students are entitled to be in control of their learning yet still need adult guidance.

7. The unique nature of the individual is valuable. The personal signature of students brings rich and wonderful diversity to classrooms.

8. When these beliefs are acted out by teachers and principals, learning will improve and ensure more success for more students than the traditional system.

Applying the philosophy

Empowerment in schools is not without its dilemmas. As schools try to employ "power with" practices, most school systems still function as "power over" systems with parents, board members, and administrators making many unilateral decisions. Within such systems, those powerful people at the top resist giving up control. Administrators and teachers will have to struggle for their own empowerment by showing those in power the ultimate advantage to students and the school system itself.

In a sense, by empowering students, teachers and principals are changing the system from the bottom up. If teachers wait until the system brings about the changes, large numbers of students will continue to leave middle schools unmotivated, ignorant, and unprepared for the rigors of high school or life.

The difficulty in implementing student empowerment stems not only from the existing power structures in school systems but also with existing models of power within schools and classrooms. Those models must be re-examined and new models created. Creating conditions for student empowerment does not require a decision between "power with" or "power over." It is not an either-or decision. Because teachers are entrusted by parents with the safety and well-being of a large number of children, it will always be necessary for teachers to maintain some power over their students. Realistically speaking, the current climate of teacher accountability necessitates some autocratic decisions on the part of the teacher.

Teachers will be expected to determine basic outcomes of instruction, custom design instruction for different types of learners, and function as priority setters and standard bearers for student work. Most importantly, teachers must create the optimum work environment for productivity and assure that some students are not allowed to interfere with the learning of others. This requires developing a sense of community within the classroom and the school, where students work together to reach both group and individual goals. Teachers will be required to meld the two concepts of power and create a hybrid power that maximizes students' control over their own learning while balancing the needs of students, the teacher, and the system.

> *If teachers wait until the system brings about the changes,*
> *large numbers of students will continue to leave*
> *middle schools unmotivated, ignorant, and*
> *unprepared for the rigors of high school or life.*

Obstacles to student empowerment

Obstacles to student empowerment are both systemic and personal. On the personal level several barriers may be found within teachers and administrators themselves. Relationships of domination not only saturate the structures and norms of schools and the experiences and expectations of students and administrators, but they also lie deep within teachers. The struggle to move beyond relationships of domination is not solely with external forces, it is an internal struggle as well. It means wrestling with long-held assumptions about teaching and shaking our taken-for-granted patterns of acting and ways of relating in classrooms (Kreisberg, 1992).

Teachers and administrators need to examine their own assumptions and analyze how the existing school system and society have contributed to those assumptions. In a society where teachers are often not respected but demeaned, teachers often feel powerless. They feel powerless to control so many aspects of their jobs, the kind of children they teach, the children's previous learning experiences and home environment, and what materials and facilities are available. Because teachers feel powerless to control so many aspects of their jobs, it is not surprising they hold on fiercely to the little power they have. Their classroom is their kingdom. In school systems where teachers have little power, the idea of giving power to students sounds like a no-win situation. In a "power over" system, relinquishing one's power is viewed as a disadvantage.

The coercive nature of schooling has conditioned teachers to believe that autocratic authority must be maintained or utter chaos will result. Strict obedience to a pervasive set of rules must be maintained regardless of the cost (Theory X Management at its worst!). This is, in fact, a false dichotomy, and a harmful one, impeding learning for many. The persistence of the punishment model of discipline hampers teachers' efforts to form meaningful, respectful relationships with students that could increase student productivity and success. How much instructional time is wasted in schools every day as teachers struggle to enforce rules about chewing gum and hats, fearful that lack of compliance will wreak havoc? Is it impossible for students to be responsible about such matters, or have they never been given the chance?

In an age of accountability teachers' fears restrict them. Worried that poor test results may endanger their jobs, teachers tightly control the curriculum and limit instruction to "teaching the test." Responsibility to "look good" on the tests creates anxiety, inhibiting creativity and risk taking. The traditional ways feel safe and secure but often produce less than hoped-for results.

> *Because teachers feel powerless to control so many aspects of their jobs, it is not surprising they hold on fiercely to the little power they have.*

Today those traditional ways work for fewer and fewer students. With so many students either failing or being only marginally successful, it is time to rethink the traditional ways. In the past, teaching has been required but learning has been optional. Those who did not learn the way the teacher taught were diagnosed as having some educational malady and separated from other learners for treatment, thereby absolving teachers and schools from responsibility for a child's failure.

Students have learned to be disempowered in the traditional system. The purpose and rationale of many traditional school practices is to control students and maintain the status quo. The messages students receive from those practices reinforce the concept that teachers don't trust students. Students have to be controlled, they must be watched. Procedures, policies, and rules are more important than people. Inherent in what teachers do and say is a clear message that they expect a certain number of students to fail and that they will let them fail. Assured that some will fail, schools establish detention programs, in-school suspension, retention, and special programs that reinforce students as failures and further disenfranchise them (Raebeck, 1992).

In many schools today, it is no longer possible for teachers to absolve themselves of the responsibility for student failure. Assessment practices are changing gradually as students are expected to show what they've learned. Performance assessment measures are forcing teachers to reach more students.

An empowered school sends different messages. There is an expectation that students will do well, develop good habits, and master learning. The maxim *all children can learn* is honored, although it is recognized that some will learn easier and faster than others. Since children learn in different ways, they require a variety of methods and paths to reach the same destination. Failure in either learning or behavior is viewed as an opportunity, not as a punishable offense. Learning is more important than test scores, and people are more important than procedures or paperwork. Figure 1(p. 10) compares traditional disempowering beliefs and practices with empowering beliefs and practices

> *Learning is more important than test scores, and people are more important than procedures or paperwork.*

Practices that empower students capitalize on what educators know about learning. Student empowerment uses knowledge about the developmental needs of young adolescents, brain-based research, motivation, learning styles, failure orientation, ability grouping, control theory, and just plain human nature. It applies what has been learned about teacher empowerment to the task of empowering students. The student is the key to transforming schools. If middle level schools are to reflect a student-centered philosophy, it seems obvious that locus of change should reside in the student. ■

Figure 1

	TRADITIONAL SCHOOL	EMPOWERING SCHOOL
Beliefs	• some can learn • teaching is telling • failure is punished	• all can learn • teaching is monitoring • failure is learning
Roles	• teacher as worker • student as product	• teacher as leader • student as worker
Practices	• learning as listening • content curriculum • standardized tests • ABCDF grading • one-chance learning • ability grouping • pull-out programs • retention • punitive discipline	• learning as doing • process curriculum • performance assessment • descriptive assessment • mastery learning • mixed ability grouping • class within a class • intensive remediation • logical consequences

Empowering Students for Academic Equity

cademic success for all students is the ultimate goal of student empowerment. Before that goal can be realized, two major factors must be dealt with – practices and attitudes.

The most formidable obstacle to student success is the pervasive practice of sorting and ranking learners (Canady & Hotchkiss, 1989). Reinforcing the belief that some students cannot learn, this practice has perpetuated a system that not only allows but actually expects failure. In far too many schools, the bell-shaped curve is the icon that dictates programs and labels the teacher or the curriculum "too easy" when enough students do not fail.

The bell-shaped curve, still considered the ideal outcome of aggregate assessment in many schools, is ultimately destructive of learning environments and the spirit of mutual improvement. The bell curve (and some other grading systems) has the effect, perhaps unintended, of setting up unnecessary and counterproductive scarcities of student success in competitive, win-lose environments (Bonstingl, 1992).

The practice of sorting and ranking students is imbedded in the traditional system. In such a system, when failure does occur, it is seen as the fault of the student and the blame is placed squarely there. There is something wrong with them; they need to be "fixed" (Glasser, 1969). Special programs are created for at-risk students to separate them from successful students. High, average, and low tracks are created under the misguided perception that such differentiated tracks will benefit students. Granted, at the extremes of the bell-shaped curve lie a small number of students with exceptional needs. For the severely handicapped and the truly gifted, some separation may be preferable. But the system works against a large group of students. Those who don't learn the same way or at the same pace as others aren't necessarily handicapped, but the system itself handicaps them by labeling them as failures.

It doesn't take long for children to find out where they fit in the five pigeonholes of the bell curve, and the student's narrow academic self-image becomes, all too often, intertwined in self-fulfilling prophecies played out throughout life (Bonstingl, 1992). Ability grouping for middle level students is especially damaging as students form identities in relation to peers and adults.

Cut off from alternative routes to competence and self-esteem and preoccupied with developing an acceptable identity, middle grades students who must repeat a grade or who are tracked into lower ability groups learn to define themselves as losers (Wheelock & Dorman, 1988).

Failure orientation in students is an insidious disease built upon from kindergarten and exacerbated by traditional practices once believed to help failing students. Recent research indicates that the impact of ability grouping on student success is largely negative (George, 1993; Oakes, 1985; Slavin, 1990). The cumulative impact of years of ability grouping on measures of student intelligence appears to be significant. (For a good synthesis of recent research, see *Educational Leadership*, October 1992, and ASCD's *Curriculum Update*, June 1993). The problems of sorting and ranking are not limited to ability grouping. They occur in grading as well. Grades and tracks not only label and separate students, they also deny some students membership in the pro-school group and force them to form their own anti-school group to meet their needs for acceptance and membership (Cusick, 1989). Only through achieving academic success are students able to gain true acceptance and membership in the pro-school group.

In spite of the research indicating negative effects, sorting and ranking practices are still alive and well in many middle level schools. If educators are to reduce the level of student failure, they must be prepared to investigate how the system itself contributes to the problem. The sorting and ranking system that handicaps some students must be eliminated and replaced with new attitudes and new methods for working positively with students.

Changing teacher beliefs

The fundamental belief that all students may be successful must be accepted by all teachers. Some teachers resist accepting this concept, pointing to their years of experience in a system that has been structured and designed to assure that some do fail. The predominant resistance among teachers is evidence of how the sorting/ranking concept permeates education. Why is it so difficult for teachers to believe that all students can learn?

> *The fundamental belief that all students may be*
> *successful must be accepted by all teachers.*

The sorting and ranking system works so easily for teachers. The teacher presents a lesson, gives an assignment or a test, grades it, and ranks the relative quality of learners. Based on how well they do, students are labeled *poor, average,* and *excellent.* A few teachers enjoy this kind of evaluation, a high level cognitive task. The hierarchy of ranked learners feels right to them, especially since many teachers were highly ranked learners when they were students. The traditional system is also comfortable for many teachers. Good teaching and years of service are often rewarded by the assignment to high track classes that are much more enjoyable than average ones. Top students have adapted well to traditional methods, while poor students seem to be unteachable by these traditional methods. Many teachers continue to assume that the ability to learn or not learn is innate and that poor students cannot learn because they have not learned. One explanation for this thinking is what Dweck (1992) calls the "entity theory of intelligence." It is the belief that intelligence is a fixed entity that a student either has or doesn't have. If teachers believe this theory, it is logical to classify students and infer innate inability. Unfortunately, this view becomes a self-fulfilling prophecy as children internalize the views they observe in adults.

Children who adhere to the entity theory think of intelligence as fixed, one either has it or doesn't have it. Consequently, each learning situation represents a test of the child's abilities; if you do well, it proves that you are smart; if you do poorly, it proves that you are not. They get these ideas from us. Adults teach children to think of intelligence as fixed and unequally distributed because that is the way the great majority of adults have been taught to think about it (Dweck, 1992).

Statements like "she's always been good at math" or "he's just not bright" attribute success and failure to the student, reinforcing the idea that intelligence is fixed. This belief dies hard, partially because teachers were probably good students, were told they were smart, and attributed their school success to innate ability. To compound the problem, their experiences as teachers in a sorting and ranking system have reinforced the belief that students come to them with a fixed intelligence. Teachers have been taught it, they believe it, and the system maintains it.

Making academic success possible

The first crucial factor in empowering academic success is the belief that success is possible. One theory favoring this stand is the incremental theory of intelligence, the idea that intelligence is built up incrementally through effort. It is possible for people to get smarter with hard work. "Smart is not something you are, smart is something you get" (Dweck, 1992, p. 31). In fact, brain-based research has shown this to be possible and that the brain "grows" new connections with new experiences (Caine & Caine, 1991). Teachers may claim to believe this but still not really believe all students can be successful. They may, for instance, point to the lack of motivation of at-risk students, and claim that no matter what they do, the students will not be able to perform. Research in at-risk behavior shows that laziness and lack of motivation are usually smoke screens or defensive mechanisms used to avoid more failure. "When young adolescents are unsure or afraid of where they're going, the safest bet is to go nowhere, the surest thing to do nothing" (Martino, 1993, p. 19). In reality, almost all at-risk middle level students want to succeed and believe with assistance they can (Ruff, 1993).

> *When young adolescents are unsure or afraid*
> *of where they're going, the safest bet is to go*
> *nowhere, the surest thing to do nothing.*

The second factor necessary for empowering academic success is the belief that teachers can substantially affect student success. Since many factors affecting learning are beyond the teacher's control, one might assume that the teacher's effect is minimal. Yet perhaps more than at any other stage of schooling, middle level teachers have tremendous power to impact learning. The impact of the teacher may, in fact, overwhelm a host of factors such as home and environment. Naturally, a wise teacher enlists the assistance of parents and community to help students succeed. However, it is counterproductive to focus the blame for student failure on parents or environment, factors that are substantially out of the school's control. Teachers and principals should not assume the child's fate is sealed by home and environment, but rather concentrate on how those obstacles can be overcome with radical treatment.

Because much about learning is still a mystery, educators may never know for sure how the complex interaction of people, processes, programs, and policies within a school impact learning. By far, the classroom teacher is the most significant factor in "inviting" school success (Purkey & Stanley, 1991). In the non-scientific laboratory of the classroom, unsure of just how much they can impact student success, teachers may fear they cannot overcome the effects of home and environment. In the past, teachers tried their best and still had students fail, a painful experience for both student and teacher. But those efforts were most likely within the traditional sorting and ranking system with staid methods. Some children may come to us so damaged by home and environment they cannot succeed; but they are few. More likely, unsuccessful students have been unwittingly damaged by precisely the educational practices created to help them. Using all the knowledge currently available, will there still be some who will not succeed? Until practices and attitudes are changed it is impossible to know. Teachers must believe in their own efficacy and instill in students a faith in their own abilities.

> *By far, the classroom teacher is the most significant factor in 'inviting' school success.*

The third factor necessary for academic empowerment is responsibility. In the past, teachers have taken responsibility for teaching, but not always for learning. In fact, it appears that students have not been required to take responsibility for learning either. The traditional method of teaching, testing, and assigning grades has made students responsible only for grades, not learning. Grades have been more important than learning. Other practices have undermined the development of responsibility within students. Teachers, in effect, allow students not to learn, not to participate. It's often easier and more energy efficient to concentrate efforts on those who appear ready to learn. Teachers often make excuses for students who don't learn and may even rescue them from failure, pain, or frustration associated with learning. Landfried (1989) called such practices "educational enabling." Students then develop "learned helplessness" and the rescue results in a drowning. Educational enabling allows teachers to rationalize student failure or rationalize acceptable grades for little effort. If all students are to learn, teachers must make a conscious effort not to allow students' problems to become excuses for failure (Taylor & Reeves, 1993). In an age of accountability, enabling is a way for teachers to protect themselves when students don't learn. In addition, the ABCDF grading system can be used to absolve teachers of responsibility for a lack of student learning. In the traditional teach, test, assign grades system, it is easy to place the blame on the students. The material was taught and the test was given, therefore all students should have learned.

> *If all students are to learn, teachers must make a conscious effort not to allow students' problems to become excuses for failure.*

"Blame is leveled by saying students 'chose' not to study or 'earned' a certain grade – conveniently removing all responsibility from educators and deflecting attention from the curriculum and the context in which it is taught" (Kohn, 1994, p. 40). In the most successful programs, teachers believe they are personally accountable for student success (Wehlage, Rutter, Smith, Lesko, & Fernandez, 1989).

Shared responsibility, shared power

In an empowered system, teachers and students share power as well as responsibility for student success and failure. In a traditional school, teachers often claim they ask students to "take responsibility" but only within the teacher's parameters and by the teacher's rules. Such is not responsibility but obedience – similar to the administrator who claims to empower teachers by allowing them to provide input, and then proceeds to ignore or neutralize their input.

Empowering students requires teachers to rethink the power structure within the classroom. Shared power and responsibility means that students are given control over their own academic futures, have input into classroom decisions, are held accountable for their actions, and are allowed to solve their own problems.

Prerequisites for academic success

Teachers are responsible not only for students' learning but for developing the prerequisites for their successful learning. Empowering for academic success means equipping students with the tools and skills that will enable them to be self-directed learners. In the past, these skills were often taught and reinforced in the home. The authority structures and rules between home and school were more consistent than they are today. Teachers, assuming students came to school with the necessary skills, did not bother to teach them. The assumption was made that those who did not have the skills must somehow have been unable to learn them, and therefore unable to learn much else.

What skills and tools are essential for school success? Each school will need to prioritize the skills and tools deemed most critical for their students. These skills and tools may be quite different from those needed to succeed in the traditional sorting and ranking system. Memorization, reading speed, and the ability to make quick decisions may no longer be as important in an empowered system that focuses on teaching and in-depth learning. Below is one list of skills and tools necessary for self-directed learning:

- Reading comprehension – making meaning from written material.
- Oral expression – the ability to express ideas clearly.
- Social skills – the ability to work productively with others.
- Question asking – the ability to make meaning from information.
- Analyzing – the ability to learn from mistakes.
- Methodical, logic-based problem solving and decision making.
- Goal setting and creating plans for reaching goals.
- Designing and evaluating one's own learning experience.

If all students are to be academically successful, schools cannot take for granted that students come to school equipped with these prerequisite skills and tools. At-risk students will require specialized academic help to overcome basic skills deficiencies. These skills should not be taught in isolation, but integrated meaningfully into content learning tasks. Teachers need to accommodate differences in skill levels and be prepared to teach and model the skills and tools for successful learning. "Not my job" many will say. Yet if the job of the teacher is learning, teachers will need to re-examine their attitudes and beliefs and revise instruction to incorporate prerequisite tools and skills into the curriculum. Many middle level students are denied access to success because they lack those prerequisite skills.

Once teachers assist students in acquiring the needed skills and tools, how will they get students to take responsibility for their own learning? Promoting responsibility requires three things: that children understand the task (which includes the scope of the job and standard for completion), accept the task, and be able to motivate oneself (Crary, 1990). The teacher's primary role is to facilitate student understanding, acceptance of responsibility, and self-motivation. The best way to accomplish that is to plan curriculum based on student needs. Glasser (1984) identified four basic human needs that are especially relevant for middle level learners: the need to belong, the need for power, the need for freedom – to make choices, and the need for fun – to enjoy the work we do. Students at this age also have strong needs for competence and achievement and for activities which promote a sense of identity. If student needs are used as a medium for developing the curriculum, students will accept responsibility for learning.

New roles for teachers

Student empowerment requires the teacher to be intensely involved in creating the right emotional climate and designing the right experiences that allow it to happen. Some flowers can grow and bloom in the wild, while others need special soil and much caretaking to thrive. The critical role of the teacher in ensuring the intellectual growth of all students cannot be underestimated. It is significantly different from the traditional role. Below are several facets of the teacher's role in a student-empowered classroom.

Climate designer. The teacher should provide a non-threatening environment for learning. A continuous progress system should provide chances for success, motivation, and meet emotional and intellectual needs for achievement and competence. Development of empowering attitudes is a critical component of climate. Students must believe tasks are within their capabilities and that adequate support will be available if help is needed (Vatterott, 1990).

Skills teacher. The teacher should provide continuous help with basic academic skills as well as social skills. They should not be taught in isolation, but should be learned within the context of tasks in which their application is immediate and compelling.

Task designer. This role probably represents the biggest challenge. Learning tasks for middle level students should be designed to meet their social and emotional needs. Tasks should require active learning, use basic skills, and as often as possible be hands-on, concrete experiences. The ideal learning task capitalizes on students' personal and social concerns and is rich in personal relevance (Beane, 1993). Whenever possible, tasks should involve performance or creation of a product. In addition, teachers will need to customize learning tasks to accommodate individual differences in learning style and speed. Block schedules or homework assignments may need to be adjusted to allow some students extra time to complete tasks. Students should be given some choices that allow them to tap their unique interests and enhance their need for identity.

Learning coach. The teacher should explain or demonstrate learning tasks to students, encouraging dialogue in the classroom, and train students to ask questions to clarify the task (Shor, 1992). Specific corrective feedback should be provided as soon as possible, and evidence of student progress should be concrete and visible. The teacher as coach pushes students to do their best and intensifies efforts when needed. Coaches also model persistence by refusing to give up on students and doing whatever is necessary to help them succeed.

Standard setter. Standards for completion imply that there is a minimum level of quality that is acceptable, as opposed to the traditional ABCDF grading system, in which almost anything is accepted and labeled as to quality (Glasser, 1990). Standards will require completion to be outcome-based, not time-based (Spady & Marshall, 1991). Standards should be clearly outlined in writing, and samples of acceptable quality should be available. This role will clearly require an assessment process different from the traditional.

To empower students, teacher time and energy must be directed away from content presentation and grading toward the customizing of learning for individuals. As students take more responsibility for their own learning, teachers will have more time to structure and individualize learning experiences. The role of the teacher must be reconceptualized as coach, facilitator, and monitor of active student learning. Curriculum emphasis must shift away from content toward process. All of this will result in redefining the teacher's role. In *Soylent Green*, an old science fiction movie, the world had been virtually destroyed. Two of the few survivors meet, and one asked another if all the books had been destroyed. She took him to the last remaining "book," which turned out to be an old man who knew a lot about one particular topic. Teachers often define themselves by their content. If students are to be responsible for their own learning, teachers can no longer be "books." Instead they will be people who facilitate learning in others.

What drives curriculum?

If students are given the tools and skills necessary to learn, if learning is designed to be active and personally relevant, and if students are given the power to design and evaluate their own learning experiences, learning will be an intrinsically pleasant experience. By capitalizing on student needs for competence and achievement, instruction will produce willing and successful learners. Changes in instruction alone, however, are irrelevant until we decide "with what curriculum and by what standards?" Success at memorizing facts will not empower students with any great satisfaction or skills to handle their future. Beane (1997) advocates a new curriculum vision that requires a significant student voice in curriculum planning. Curriculum themes and activities should emerge from concerns of students rather than the interests of the teacher. In a student-focused curriculum, students learn by constructing knowledge and take pride in creating products that demonstrate that knowledge.

A student-focused classroom requires a different relationship between curriculum and instruction. Curriculum and instruction are inextricably tied; it serves no purpose to discuss curriculum without exploring its relationship to instruction. In a traditional teacher-focused classroom, the teacher retains all power and makes all decisions. Curriculum (content) dictates instruction. Content is something the teacher knows that the student does not, and the teacher decides what is worth knowing. Knowledge is power and the teacher has it. Instruction consists of "covering" the content, and students are graded on how much of it they "got," however temporarily. Teaching is required, but learning is optional.

A student-focused classroom requires a fundamental shift in what drives curriculum and instruction. Student interests and questions determine the curriculum, and student goals and needs become the starting point that directs instruction. Curriculum (content) becomes the end result, not the beginning. The goal of the teacher is to meet the learning goals of students. Instruction is what the teacher does to facilitate learning. Instruction is no longer "done to" but becomes the creation of a "place to learn." Knowledge is defined as the ability to do something, not recite something. Perhaps it could be illustrated thus: *universal goals for all students*, planned around the *needs of particular students,* result in *individual adaptations* and *individualized content*, that defines the content of the curriculum.

> *In a student-focused curriculum, students learn by constructing knowledge and take pride in creating products that demonstrate that knowledge.*

This does not mean students share no common curriculum. The universal goals are the common curriculum. The content of the curriculum is gained through the processes designed to reach universal goals. In other words, students experience unique content on their journeys to common goals. The teacher's focus is on goal setting not content coverage. Obviously, if all students are to achieve the same goals, the student-focused curriculum will require an assessment system more like performance assessment. The traditional ABCDF grading system is inappropriate.

Empowering students for academic success will require major changes in practices and attitudes. The system must move from a sorting and ranking system to a teaching and learning system (Canady & Hotchkiss, 1989). The nature of the curriculum and its relationship to student needs must be re-examined. Universal goals for all students must drive the curriculum. All students must be provided the skills for self-directed learning.

Systems cannot change until attitudes change. Teachers must believe in their own ability to impact student learning and the student's will to learn. Teachers must learn to share power and responsibility with their students and adopt new roles to facilitate the process of student empowerment. ■

Creating a Supportive Learning Community

A nurturing and supportive classroom environment is essential for the intellectual as well as the emotional and social development of young adolescents. Although some students can be academically successful in spite of non-supportive conditions, for many students an unsupportive climate can exacerbate academic failure. For some time evidence has existed to prove that a supportive classroom climate not only increases student efforts and academic motivation (Johnston & Markle, 1986), but also improves achievement (Jensen, 1998). The critical link between attitude and academic performance is especially evident with middle school students, whose psychological and emotional states are so fragile.

"If you want academic excellence, you have to attend to how children feel about school and about each other" (Kohn, 1996, p.103). For many students, emotional and social needs are so preeminent, learning is simply not a priority. These children need help with their emotional and social development; they need to learn how to be productive citizens. The classroom, the team, and the school that function like a democratic community teach valuable social and emotional lessons while providing a fertile environment for academic success. The environment that helps young adolescents develop emotionally and socially also enhances learning.

Developmental needs the classroom environment should address

Although young adolescents have many developmental needs, those described by Erikson are particularly germane to issues of student empowerment. According to Erikson (1963), young adolescents struggle to resolve two developmental conflicts: *industry vs. inferiority* – the need for competence and achievement; and *identity vs. role confusion* – the need to define oneself and to develop appropriate roles. Those two conflicts encompass other needs that, when met, will assist young adolescents in their personal and social development.

Industry vs. inferiority

In resolving the conflict of industry and inferiority, young adolescents ask, "Am I a good person?" "What am I good at?" To help in answering these questions, middle level students need opportunities to identify and solve problems, complete tasks, and set and reach goals. They need knowledge about the world around them to make sense of it. They need to discover what they are good at and be recognized for it (Scales, 1991). In order for students to experience competence, they must be given the power to make decisions directly. We should examine every aspect of life in the classroom and consider what decisions might be turned over to students (Kohn, 1996). This requires a shift in the way teachers and students interact, from "doing to" power to "working with" power within the classroom.

> *Every aspect of life in the classroom should cause us to reflect on what decisions might be turned over to students.*

The difficulty of relinquishing power, or even realizing the importance of doing so, is evident from the number of adults who spend their days ordering children around, complaining all the while that "kids just don't take responsibility for their own behavior." The truth is that if we want children to "take" responsibility, we must first "give" them responsibility, and plenty of it (Kohn, 1996). Needs of competence and achievement can be addressed by giving students responsibility within the classroom and through curricular and instructional designs, especially those that facilitate academic success for all students (this topic is discussed in Chapter 4). The development of a sense of competence and achievement plays an important role in the development of the young adolescent's personal and social identity.

Identity vs. role confusion

In resolving the conflict of identity and role confusion, the young adolescent struggles to define his/her personal identity (*Who am I?*) and a social identity (*How am I perceived by others?*). The search for personal identity could best be described as the search for a unique sense of self, independent of family. However, most adolescents attempt to reconcile that identity with family identity, simultaneously needing both independence and acceptance from their family. Personal identity is also related to young adolescents' need for industry as they attempt to develop a positive self image (*Am I a good person?*). The search for a unique sense of self creates a strong need for acceptance. In forming their personal identity, young adolescents try to integrate role model ideals into their own sense of self and their own unique value system (Manning, 1993). Obviously, young adolescents benefit from adult role models in the classroom. More importantly, classroom opportunities for creative self-expression, self-definition, and reflection are helpful as young adolescents develop their personal identity (Scales, 1991).

In their search for personal identity, young adolescents need both individuality and group membership. They want to be accepted as the unique persons they are, yet they also want to belong to a group. The creation of a caring community within the classroom and team provides a healthy, wholesome way for young adolescents to belong. The identification with a group, one's role in society, and one's acceptance by others all serve to further define individual identity. Social identity is influenced by needs for love and belonging, beyond what family can provide. Acceptance (*People like me just the way I am.*) and membership (*I'm part of a group; we are family.*) are critical to the development of identity and a positive self-concept in young adolescents. It is through the integration of the many influences in their lives (peers, family, and other adults) that young adolescents integrate their identity with a group identity.

In their search for personal identity, young adolescents have simultaneous needs for individuality and group membership.

When students' needs for belonging and membership are not met by teachers and students, they are at risk of academic failure. They feel "disconnected" from the school (Strahan, 1989), and that sense of disconnectedness produces apathy (Wehlage et al., 1989).

When students have little attachment to teachers and administrators, they do not care what these people think about them, especially in their role as students. In return, students perceive that these adults do not care about them. Under these conditions, students feel disengaged from the school and may chose to leave (Arhar, 1992).

> *When students have little attachment to teachers and administrators, they do not care what these people think about them, especially in their role as students.*

In other words, if students perceive that adults and other students do not care about them, then the students decide not to care what these adults think about them. The students put forth little effort to learn because effort may result in failure. Disconnected students do not want to risk failure if they feel they have no support – much like walking a tightrope without a safety net. It's much easier not to try. This apathy results in less effort, which causes poor performance, which in turn produces a lack of teacher motivation to continue to meet student needs. This lack of teacher involvement fuels further student apathy (Vatterott, 1991).

A supportive classroom environment can break that cycle by creating a place where students feel personally connected to teachers, other students, and to the school as a family. This connectedness, or social bonding, has been shown to be an important factor in student motivation (Arhar, 1992). In fact, brain research has shown that positive social feedback actually increases certain chemicals in the brain that make us feel good (Jensen, 1998).

What does a supportive environment feel like to students?

A supportive classroom environment is safe. A safe classroom is a place where students feel physically safe and secure, protected from physical danger. That danger could be as innocuous as a shove from another student or as foreboding as the presence of a gun or knife. Safety is the obligation of everyone in the school – principals, teachers, counselors, secretaries, custodians, and students. Safety requires a comprehensive effort by the entire school population working in conjunction with the community-at-large of families, churches, police, and social agencies.

A non-violent school is created by developing a caring community with all people in the school, cultivating non-violence as a school value, and being concerned about the mental health of everyone in the school community, both children and adults. Curwin and Mendler (1997) suggest that schools begin creating that climate by:

- identifying the core values of the school,
- creating rules and consequences using these values,
- modeling the values during interactions with students and staff,
- eliminating interventions that violate the core values. (p. 23)

Conflict resolution and other types of violence prevention programs have proven useful in some schools, but prevention-only programs have not been as effective as comprehensive programs that also address climate and relationships. The best violence prevention is a warm, nurturing environment that keeps kids close. It goes without saying that students should feel secure about their physical safety. Less obvious is the student's need for emotional safety, to be safe from ridicule and embarrassment. Most teachers prohibit students from threatening or embarrassing others but may fail to protect students from embarrassment in the learning process. A safe classroom is a non-threatening environment for learning. Students who feel safe and supported are more willing to take the risk of learning. The safety to take risks results in more effort, which in turn results in higher achievement.

> *Students who feel safe and supported are*
> *more willing to take the risk of learning.*

According to Sizer (1992) the tone of the classroom should be one of trust and fairness – "I won't threaten you, but I expect much of you." The goal is "low anxiety and high standards" (Barth, 1990). Research suggests that learning suffers when the learner's anxiety is high, that similar internal reactions occur for all kinds of threats, be they physical or psychological (Jensen, 1998).

Removing threat from the classroom is one of the most important ways teachers can create a safe learning environment. Threats of detention, lowered grades, intimidation, embarrassment, or loss of school privileges are counterproductive to learning. "Threats activate defense mechanisms and behaviors that are great for survival but lousy for learning" (Jensen, 1998, p. 57).

A supportive classroom environment is affirming

An affirming climate sends a message of teacher efficacy, the teacher's belief in his or her ability to influence student motivation and achievement. Dr. Hank Levin (in Brandt, 1992), speaking of the highly successful Accelerated Schools model, stated "the way you define children has an awful lot to do with the way you work with them" (p. 20). An affirming teacher communicates his or her belief that all students can be successful and are worthy of respect. There are no "bad kids." Students with problems such as Attention Deficit Disorder, learning disabilities, behavioral, or emotional problems are just as capable of learning as other students, given the proper conditions. At-risk students can be successful, and the teacher's belief in that success is a critical factor in overcoming failure orientation (Wehlage, et al., 1989). Students' beliefs about themselves and their learning have a major influence on their ability to learn (Jensen, 1998).

Teachers should establish themselves from the beginning as the students' allies, adults with whom they can work to solve the problems that emerge during the normal course of development.

An affirming environment does not mean children are continually praised and rewarded, but that they are given unconditional support, unconditional positive regard. Johnston (1992) calls it "pervasive caring" where people "are alert to each other's needs and take care of them without fanfare" (p.87). A caring environment sends three messages: you are valuable, you are able, and you are responsible (Strahan, 1994).

Warm, caring, empathic adults do several things at once. They provide the child with a benevolent, safe place in which to act. Kohn (1991) has made a related point in this statement:

> ...I hope that few educators take seriously the absurd dictum that teachers should display no warmth until well into the school year – after firm control of the classroom has been won. Instead, teachers should establish themselves from the beginning as the students' allies, adults with whom they can work to solve the problems that emerge during the normal course of development. (p. 503)

An affirming climate respects the dignity of students and assumes they are capable of acting responsibly. Many traditional classroom practices do not respect even the most basic of human needs. The practice of forcing students to sit in a certain position for long periods of time and not allowing them to use the restroom or get a drink ignores some of their most basic physical needs. How many adults would find such rules acceptable in their own work environments? Restricting students from moving, getting a drink, or using the restroom also reflects a mistrust of students to act responsibly.

> The fact that some child might take advantage of the chance to decide when to go to the bathroom is no justification for requiring everyone to ask permission. If it's useful to keep track of who's out of the room, or to limit the number who are gone at any given time, children can take a pass or sign out when they feel the need. Better yet, they can be asked as a class to invent a system that addresses everyone's concerns – theirs for autonomy, and the teacher's for structure or limits (Kohn, 1996, pp. 85-86).

In addition to being inconsiderate, such practices are physiologically indefensible, based on new knowledge about the brain. Factors affecting the body's physical workings (such as sleep, nutrition, and exercise) are now known to significantly influence brain chemistry. One researcher suggests that drinking water may actually enhance the brain's efficiency in learning:

> Dehydration is a common problem that's linked to poor learning. To be at their best, learners need water. If water is available in the learning environment, the typical hormone response to the stress (elevated levels of corticoids) is "markedly reduced or absent" [Levine & Coe, 1989]. These studies suggest a strong role for water in keeping learners' stress levels in check (Jensen, 1998, p. 26).

Although it may be difficult to accept the proposition that all learners need water to learn, if this is true for even some students, isn't it logical to make that accommodation available for any student who needs it? Jensen also believes that providing oxygen to the brain through fresh air, movement within the classroom, and regular physical education are important ways to enhance the brain's ability to learn.

If we trust that students want to learn and allow them to have input into how they learn, they will tell us what they need to be able to learn.

A supportive climate is interactive

Kohn (1991) noted that the interaction of the teacher and the student is rarely seen as integral to the process of learning. At the middle school level, however, interaction between the teacher and the student is pivotal in the creation of a supportive climate. If students are to feel accepted, teachers must first and foremost have regular, positive interactions with all students in their classrooms. All children are entitled to absolute positive regard whether they are dirty, poorly dressed, mean-spirited, ugly, or poor. In one disturbing study, Waxman, Huang, and Padron (1995) discovered a pattern among teachers in inner-city middle schools of minimal interactions with students.

> Teachers in this study were observed spending very little time interacting with students regarding personal issues, encouraging students to succeed, showing personal regard for students, or showing interest in students' work. These are all areas that have been found to be important for developing positive learning environments where students will become successful learners. (pp. 13-14)

These findings were similar to those from other studies of urban schools (Johnston, 1992). Personal interactions with students send powerful messages to students about themselves. Do those interactions affirm a student's sense of acceptance and membership or negate it? Do students feel respected as individuals worthy of having their needs met? Is there true teacher-student dialogue, or does all information flow only from the teacher to the student?

In addition to creating a climate that is safe, affirming, and interactive, care must be taken to directly address student needs for personal and social identity. This requires a personalized classroom climate that provides the student with a sense of security about self and a sense of group membership.

Personalizing the climate: Accommodating diversity in learners

A personalized climate seeks to validate the individuality of learners. Even though young adolescents share many similarities, as a group they are best defined by their variability. Accepting that diversity compels teachers to understand differences among learners. As individuals, young adolescents are more different than alike. Physically, the timing of the changes of puberty may create a developmental span of as much as five years between early and late developers of the same age. In other words, some students may be well into puberty by the time they enter middle school while others may leave middle school before they enter puberty. Diversity is equally evident in emotional, social, and intellectual development. Some students will be quite child-like in their leisure interests and interactions with others, yet other students will seem quite precocious. Intellectually, most are still operating at the concrete stage of development, yet some will have the ability to think abstractly. The ability for abstract thought will differ further within individuals. For example, a student may be able to understand abstract problems in algebra, yet not understand abstract concepts in another area such as social studies (Van Hoose & Strahan, 1988).

In addition to the variability brought about by the changes of puberty, middle level students also differ in the way they learn. Research on learning styles, multiple intelligences, field dependence/field independence, and brain hemisphericity has shown that students have a predominant style or method in which they learn best. Dunn and Dunn's research (1978) on learning styles indicates that students differ in four key dimensions: environment, emotional support, sociological composition, and personal/physical elements. Components of the dimensions are listed briefly in Figure 1.

Figure 1

Dunn and Dunn's Learning Styles	
DIMENSION	ELEMENTS
Environment	sound light temperature seating design
Emotional Support	motivational support persistence structure individual responsibility
Sociological Support	individual pairs or teams adult varied
Personal/Physical	modality (visual, auditory, tactile, or kinesthetic) time mobility

Environmental differences included preferences for soft or bright lighting, quiet or noise, and formal or informal seating. In the area of emotional support, students differ in their ability to be self-directed, with some students needing more support and structure than others. Sociologically, some students prefer to learn alone, some prefer learning in groups, and others prefer learning from an adult. Learning modality preferences may be auditory, visual, tactile, or kinesthetic. Some students learn better in the morning, some in the afternoon, and some students need to move more often than others. Numerous studies have found that student achievement increases when teaching methods match their learning styles (Dunn, Beaudry, & Klavas, 1989).

Gardner's research (1983) on multiple intelligences indicates that people show an inclination to develop strengths in seven different "intelligences": Linguistic, logical-mathematical, spatial, bodily-kinesthetic, musical, interpersonal, and intrapersonal. Students who have strong tendencies in specific intelligences, similar to learning styles, prefer specific kinds of learning tasks. A summary of those preferences is shown in Figure 2.

Figure 2

Summary of the "Seven Ways of Teaching"

INTELLIGENCE	TEACHING ACTIVITIES (EXAMPLES)	TEACHING MATERIALS (EXAMPLES)	INSTRUCTIONAL STRATEGIES
Linguistic	• lectures • discussions • word games • storytelling • choral reading • journal writing	• books • tape recorders • typewriters • stamp sets • books on tape	• read about it • write about it • talk about it • listen to it
Logical-Mathematical	• brain teasers • problem solving • science experiments	• calculators • math manipulatives • science equipment • math games	• quantify it • think critically about it • conceptualize it

(Figure 2, continued)

Intelligence	Teaching Activities (examples)	Teaching Materials (examples)	Instructional Strategies
Spatial	• visual presentations • art activities • imagination games • mind-mapping • metaphor • visualization	• graphs • maps • video • LEGO sets • art materials • optical illustions • cameras • picture library	• see it • draw it • visualize it • color it • mind-map it
Bodily-Kinesthetic	• hands-on learning • drama • dance • sports that teach • tactile activities • relaxation • exercises	• building tools • clay • sports equipment • manipulatives • tactile learning resources	• build it • act it out • touch it • get a "gut feeling" • dance it
Musical	• superlearning • rapping • songs that teach	• tape recorder • tape collection • musical instruments	• sing it • rap it • listen to it
Interpersonal	• cooperative learning • peer tutoring • community involvement • social gatherings • simulations	• board games • party supplies • props for role plays	• teach it • collaborate on it • interact with respect to it
Intrapersonal	• individualized instruction • independent study • options in course of study • self-esteem building	• self-checking materials • journals • materials for projects	• connect it to your personal life • make choices with regard to it

(Armstrong, 1994)

Students also differ in their tendency to be either field-dependent or field-independent learners. Field-dependent learners perceive whole patterns rather than parts, tend to be people-oriented, and work well in groups. Field-independent learners are more analytical, perceive separate parts of a whole, are task-oriented, and enjoy working alone (Johnston, 1994). Research shows that many at-risk students, as high as 85% in one study (Johnston, 1994), learn in a field-dependent modality, a style seldom found in traditional instruction, which is often field-independent and predominantly left brain. See Figure 3 for characteristics of field-dependent and field-independent learners.

Figure 3

Learning Preferences		
	FIELD DEPENDENT	FIELD INDEPENDENT
Setting	cooperative loose structure informal	formal structured individual
Focus	concepts general principles	information details
Social	work together to benefit group	work alone everyone for him/herself
Reward	for effort group contribution common good	for outcome quality of completed product on predetermined standards
Success	helping group getting group approval	meeting standard getting approval of authority

(Johnston, 1994)

Theories about right and left brain dominance show similar characteristics. Field dependence is similar to right brain dominant, global
tendencies, while field independence is similar to left brain, analytical
tendencies. The inattention to individual differences is especially evident in the experiences of at-risk students at the middle level. How
they differ in learning style from successful students may be what contributes most to their academic problems. For instance, when right brain
dominance and characteristics of certain learning styles are clustered
within individual students, what emerges is a profile of a learner out of
sync with the traditional classroom environment:

> Students who were less motivated than their classmates
> and who preferred distractors (music, low illumination,
> informal or casual seating, peers rather than alone or with
> the teacher, tactile rather than auditory or visual instruc-
> tional resources) scored right-hemisphere significantly
> more often than left-hemisphere... Left-hemisphere young-
> sters in grades 5-12 preferred a conventional formal class-
> room seating design, more structure, less intake, and vi-
> sual rather than tactile or kinesthetic resources during learn-
> ing significantly more often that their right-preferred
> classmates. (Dunn et al., 1989, p. 51)

Given this great diversity in the manner individual students learn,
the case for student choice in learning becomes more compelling. Respect for individual differences in learning impacts how lessons are
designed and how tasks are evaluated. In a personalized environment,
different or creative ways of completing the same assignment are encouraged. Honoring those differences has a significant impact on instruction, which is discussed more completely in Chapter 4.

Promoting group membership in a communal climate

In addition to the need for personalized attention and unconditional
acceptance, young adolescents need a sense of membership, of being
accepted by a group. Membership is of critical importance for middle
level students as they are faced with developmental changes and the
formation of identity. Identity involves not only personal, but social
identity, which requires positive interaction with peers to develop. It is
no wonder that the peer group is elevated to such importance by young
adolescents. After all, being accepted by a group is validation of one's

personal identity, validation that one is a "good person." Young adolescents define themselves by their group membership (Milgram, 1985). As they struggle to define themselves, their fickle attractions to various peer groups is understandable. The practice of associating and disassociating with different peer groups and cliques is a visible indicator of "trying on" different identities.

Not only is social membership important to young adolescents, but studies indicate the quality of social relationships at school may impact whether students come to school and what they will learn. At the middle level, school membership is viewed as a necessary foundation for personal and social development as well as academic achievement (Wehlage et al., 1989).

For at-risk students in particular, with backgrounds of school failure and little support from homes and communities outside the school, a strong sense of membership is essential to persistence in school. When identification with social institutions outside of the school is weakened, membership in school becomes particularly critical for adolescent development into adulthood (Arhar, 1992).

Just as membership needs can affect academic success, academic success brings acceptance as a member of a learning community, and a sense of membership in the school. Conversely, when students are not successful academically, they can't view themselves as members of the learning community. They feel disconnected and drop out, either physically or symbolically by creating their own anti-school groups (Cusick, 1989). They find other ways to meet their needs for acceptance and membership, sometimes in dangerous or anti-social ways such as gangs.

Creating a community to meet membership needs

The development of stable, close, and respectful relationships within a learning community thus becomes a key factor in the personal growth of young adolescents (Carnegie Council on Adolescent Development, 1989). Middle level students simply need to belong to a caring community. Barth (1990) popularized the concept of a "community of learners" defined as "a place where students and adults alike are engaged as active learners in matters of special importance to them and where everyone is thereby encouraging everyone else's learning" (p. 9). Kohn (1996) defined such a community as:

...a place in which students feel cared about and are encouraged to care about each other. They experience a sense of being valued and respected; the children matter to one another and to the teacher. They have come to think in the plural: they feel connected to each other; they are part of an 'us.' (p. 101)

A caring community can be created at several levels. The classroom can be a community, so can a team, a grade level, or even the entire school. At the middle school, interdisciplinary teaming provides an organizational framework for the creation of a learning community. Teaming creates conditions that facilitate social bonding (Arhar, 1992) so students feel less isolated and get to know each other better.

The team constitutes an extended family of sorts within which students can form primary social affiliations... At its best, the team serves as a positive answer for students' need to belong to a sanctioned and defined social group. (George, Stevenson, Thomason, & Beane, 1992, p. 59)

Simply placing students and teachers together in teams, however, does not guarantee that a learning community will develop. What makes a group of people a community? In a community people have input about things that affect them, people agree on the rules that will govern them, they share common goals and values, and they cooperate to reach common goals. A classroom community participates in shared decision making, answering the question, "How do we want our classroom to be?" A classroom community allows for student membership, ownership, and governance of the classroom. At the middle level, a caring community not only meets needs of young adolescents for identity and membership but has great potential as a context in which students can acquire positive moral attitudes and social skills (Kohn, 1991).

A classroom community participates in shared decision making, answering the question, "How do we want our classroom to be?"

The team of teachers is the cornerstone of that community. Several issues must be resolved to begin the process of creating a learning community. The teachers must first define themselves as a teaching community and build structures that allow a learning community to evolve and function. George and associates (1992) suggest some of the tasks teams must address in this process:

1. The team of teachers must come to agreement about their common beliefs, goals, and standards. These should be clearly spelled out in some form of written document.

2. Procedures should be determined for decision making among the team of teachers, as well as procedures for students so they may participate democratically in the decision-making process.

3. The team must make organizational decisions about roles and responsibilities of the team members and how the day-to-day schedule will be used to facilitate such things as common planning time, regrouping of students, and curriculum integration.

4. Communication networks must be established to keep administrators, parents, and students informed of team activities.

Community builds slowly. Teachers can't just go in one day and create it. It takes time for people to come to know and trust one another. The nuance of community comes from an image, a message, that builds in each student's head, one interaction, one practice at a time. Students get dozens of messages each day that either reinforce that they are members of a community or that they are not. Unwittingly, many traditional classroom and school practices impede membership and send the wrong messages to specific groups of students. Any practice that ranks or labels students has the potential to create members and non-members of the community. Some school practices that discourage membership for some students include:

- **The "star system."** Any program in which only a small number of students are chosen to get "star billing" discourages membership. Competitive sports teams where only the best athletes get to play or competitive cheerleading tryouts send a message to students that they are not part of that group (Van Hoose & Strahan, 1988).

- **"Quiet rules."** Rules which restrict students from talking in the hall, at lunch, or on the bus inhibit normal social interaction for young adolescents. For some students, this interferes with the fragile development of friendships.

- **Punitive discipline.** Discipline which causes something unpleasant to happen to a student, that seeks to embarrass or humiliate students in front of their peers is counterproductive to membership. Punishment often provokes resistance and resentment that may be taken out on peers and spoils the rapport between teacher and student (Kohn, 1993). It often causes a desire for revenge on the group and distances the offender from the other students. Discipline that consistently removes students from the classroom or the school (such as in-school suspension), further alienates students from the group and gives them fewer opportunities to bond with their age-mates.

- **Pull-out programs.** Pull-out programs for special education that consistently remove students from the learning community cause students to feel less a member. In addition, when they return to the classroom, they have missed sharing in other experiences of the group.

- **Competitive grading**. When students are forced to compete for a limited number of good grades or rewards for the best performance, the sense of community suffers. Competition interferes with performance as well as personal relationships (Kohn, 1993). Grading which sorts and ranks learners quickly causes students to self-group into the "good students" and the "bad students." Even honor rolls create a division between honor students and others.

Practices such as these make certain segments of the student population feel disconnected, to feel as if they don't belong. On the other hand, practices that send positive messages and facilitate membership include cooperative learning and peer tutoring. Alternatives to punitive discipline, such as peer counseling or peer mediation programs, help students to solve problems with less separation from the group. Classroom meetings are useful to involve all students in solving problems that affect the group. Extracurricular programs that allow all students to participate, such as intramurals or all-play sports teams, encourage a feeling of community for all students. Examples of several specific programs are listed in Chapter 5.

Sending empowering messages through practices and programs

Creating a caring community requires more than just caring. Most teachers and principals care about students. What is critical is how the message of caring is communicated. Student perceptions of school rules and common practices influence feelings about acceptance and membership. By being aware of what students perceive as caring, teachers and administrators can create an environment where students thrive (Vatterott, 1991). Students who feel they belong to a learning community share basic attitudes or beliefs about their school and the people in it. By examining those beliefs, educators gain some insight into practices that reflect an accepting and communal climate.

Figure 4 lists student beliefs, attitudes, and behaviors that relate to the basic needs of acceptance and membership. Some specific school practices that reinforce such beliefs in the students' minds are also listed.

The examples listed in Figure 4 illustrate attitudes and practices that communicate the message of pervasive caring. These school practices, and others like them, provide opportunities for students to meet their emotional needs in healthy, positive ways, rather than in negative ways. The list also reflects teacher behaviors. Teacher behavior is by far the most influential factor in creating student beliefs and behaviors that enhance feelings of acceptance and membership.

As we assess our school environment to determine its effect on students, we must ask ourselves two questions: *What practices in our schools encourage students to believe they are accepted and part of a group? What practices discourage such beliefs?* Actions often speak louder than words. Schools that struggle to meet the emotional needs of their students visibly practice what they preach. ■

Figure 4

Need: Acceptance

Student attitudes and beliefs	School practices
Students believe teachers like them.	Students have opportunities to "show off" special talents and skills.
Students believe the school is for "people like me."	Students are encouraged to share their opinions.
Students believe mistakes will be forgiven.	Teachers do not allow students to ridicule others.
Students believe their opinions are valued.	At-risk students are assigned to advisers for one-on-one help.
Students feel comfortable expressing feelings.	Teachers accommodate different learning styles.
Students believe they are some teacher's "favorite kid."	Teachers treat all students with equal respect.

Need: Membership

Student attitudes and beliefs	School practices
Students can name friends in the school setting.	Opportunities are given for teachers and students to socialize outside class.
Students socialize with other students outside of school.	Multiple types of non-academic activities are available for students (games, contests, etc.).
Students identify themselves as members of a school-sponsored group (team, club, etc.).	A large number of students participate in co-curricular activities.
Students can name someone they could discuss confidential problems with at school.	Teachers and students proudly display "badges of membership."
Students believe they are missed when absent.	Teachers are knowledgeable about individual students' interests.

(Vatterott, 1991)

IV

Student-Focused Curriculum and Instruction

Learning is a student's choice – and some choose not to learn when faced with curriculum that seems irrelevant to their everyday lives. If curriculum and instruction are designed with student needs in mind, it is more likely that students will be motivated to participate (Glasser, 1984). Middle level students need and seek the power to succeed in learning. They want more control over their learning, and they value opportunities for input and decision making in the classroom (Kramer, 1992). Activities that foster student choice, alternatives, and autonomy meet developmental needs and are motivating to students (Thomason & Thompson, 1992).

Disturbingly, however, the trend in many intermediate schools is to give less responsibility, choice, and freedom to students than they had in upper elementary school (Thomason & Thompson, 1992). In many middle level schools today, traditional teacher-focused instruction inhibits students from meeting their developmental needs:

> For example, at this age, students' abilities to reason, integrate, and evaluate information burgeon, yet many school tasks are repetitive and rote, requiring only low-level cognitive processes. At the same time, middle grades students are developing a greater desire for autonomy and independence, yet many instructional practices are tightly controlled...Although such practices may maintain order, they risk losing a great deal more: young students' involvement in and commitment to learning. (Turner & Meyer, 1995, p. 18)

To meet their needs for industry and identity, students need a system that gives them more control over their learning and more independence as learners. To create such a system requires teachers to give up a certain amount of control over curriculum and instructional methods. "A curriculum geared to the needs of learners requires of the teacher an

43

enormous amount of flexibility, a high tolerance for unpredictability, and a willingness to give up absolute control of the classroom" (Kohn, 1993, p. 217). Just as parents of young adolescents struggle to balance limits with freedom, and eventually allow their children to be independent, so must middle school teachers. If teachers want students to become self-directed learners, they must be willing to allow them some input, choices, and autonomy. Student-focused instruction is a means of providing students with that autonomy.

Student-focused instruction: Shared responsibility, shared power

In student-focused instruction, teachers and students share responsibility for student success and failure. Students have input into classroom decisions, are held accountable for their actions and are allowed to solve their own problems. Students have some control over the how, when, and why of tasks and assignments. Kohn (1996) characterizes a learner-centered classroom as one where teachers "work with" students rather than doing things "to" students. To understand how student-focused instruction differs from traditional teacher-focused instruction, it may be helpful to compare the two types of instruction (Figure 1).

Teacher-focused instruction closely resembles the traditional, didactic instruction many of us experienced in elementary and high school. All content is chosen by the teacher, and most often delivered in direct instruction by lecturing or asking students questions. Teacher talk predominates with little student talk. Curriculum is typically organized part-to-whole. Activities rely heavily on textbooks and workbooks, and assessment is viewed as separate from learning.

Student-focused instruction is best typified by Beane's model (1993), in which curriculum topics are generated by student questions, learning takes place whole-to-part with an emphasis on big concepts, and the learning activity is often the assessment. Student-focused instruction shares many qualities with constructivism. Constructivism, a theory developed from research in cognitive psychology, has most often been applied in the field of early childhood education. However, the developmental and child-centered nature of constructivism makes many aspects of it applicable to adolescents as well. Philosophically, constructivism draws heavily from the work of Piaget (1954) who believed that learning occurs through the child's interaction with the environment. According to constructivist theory, cognitive development

Figure 1

Differences Between
Teacher-Focused and Student-Focused Instruction

TEACHER-FOCUSED INSTRUCTION	STUDENT-FOCUSED INSTRUCTION
Curriculum is presented part-to-whole, with emphasis on basic skills.	Curriculum is presented whole-to-part with emphasis on big concepts.
Strict adherence to fixed curriculum is highly valued.	Pursuit of student questions is highly valued.
All content decisions made by teacher.	Students are allowed to make some content decisions.
Teacher asks questions of students.	Students generate questions they want answers to.
Curricular activities rely heavily on textbooks and workbooks.	Curricular activities rely heavily on primary sources of data and manipulative materials.
Teacher generally behaves in a didactic manner, disseminating information to students.	Teacher generally behaves in an interactive manner, mediating the environment for students.
Teacher talks to teach.	Students talk to learn.
Assessment of student learning is viewed as separate from teaching and occurs almost entirely through testing.	Assessment of student learning is interwoven with teaching and occurs through teacher observation...student exhibitions and portfolios.
Written tests determine what students learn.	Projects require learning to complete.
Learning activity is different from the test.	Learning activity is often the assessment.

in young children is a result of individual constructions of meaning made by the learner (DeVries & Kohlberg, 1987). Children do not acquire knowledge through the mimetic approaches of committing information to short-term memory and mimicking an understanding of it on a test. Instead, they gain understanding by making connections of new concepts to existing structures of knowledge, thus constructing their own meaning. The child's interests and prior experiences become the "fuel" of the constructive process (Piaget, 1970). Brain-based research confirms that the desire to make meaning is innate and that emotion, relevance, and the creation of organizing patterns contribute to meaning making (Jensen, 1998).

> *Brain-based research confirms that the desire to make meaning is innate and that emotion, relevance, and the creation of organizing patterns contribute to meaning-making*

The belief that the nature of learning is an internal construction of knowledge leads to what Brooks and Brooks (1993) call "honoring the learning process." If teachers respect the worth of a child's existing knowledge and experience, they will use it as they plan learning activities.

Changing relationships and roles

The goal of student-focused instruction is to move the student toward becoming a self-directed learner. Promising examples of this concept have emerged in the Coalition of Essential Schools based on the work of Ted Sizer.

The governing metaphor of the school should be student-as-worker, rather than the much more familiar metaphor of teacher-as-deliverer-of-instructional-services. A prominent pedagogy will be coaching, to learn *how* to learn and thus to teach themselves (Sizer, 1992). In Coalition schools, the old roles of teacher as worker and student as product are abandoned in favor of the new roles of teacher as leader and student as worker. "The teacher's role, meanwhile, has shifted from a provider of information to someone who helps guide students through exploration and discovery" (Keller, 1995, p. 11).

Teachers are responsible for creating the environment, attitudes, and working conditions necessary for self-directed learners. The more tightly controlled students have been in the past, the more difficult self-direction will be. "The more they are controlled, the more they come to need control and the less they have the chance to take responsibility for their own learning and behavior" (Kohn, 1993, p. 154). Controlling techniques are most often used with special education students, exacerbating their ability to self-regulate (Kohn, 1993). It is no surprise that the lack of independent learning behaviors and the inability to make choices are common in special education students. Students who lack experience in self-directed learning and decision making because it has not been required of them in the past will need training and time to learn how to learn independently. "Empowerment with responsibility" is one of the underlying principles of accelerated schools (Keller, 1995). Students as workers are responsible for their learning. The development of that responsibility is a three-step process: first comes choice, then ownership, and finally empowerment (Scott, 1994). Student choice involves consequences, and teachers and students will make mistakes and bad choices.

Students who lack experience in self-directed learning and decision making because it has not been required of them in the past will need training and time to learn how to learn independently.

But as students cope with these problems, with teacher support, they will learn how to handle them and will develop responsibility. The students certainly can't learn responsibility if they are never given any. As the teacher lets go, students use their own choices more and more successfully. As ownership is achieved and responsibility is exercised, students become empowered. They have gained control of a part of their learning (Scott, 1994).

In student-focused instruction students are active, constructing their own knowledge, making their own learning, and assessing their own learning. The way students interact with the curriculum becomes as important as students' interaction with the teacher. The role of the teacher is to mediate the student and the curriculum, acting as coach, facilitator, and monitor.

The change in the relationships among teacher, students, and curriculum and assessment can be conceptualized using the following analogies: In the traditional teacher-focused classroom, the teacher transfers the curriculum content to the student, much like a person pouring beans (the curriculum) into a jar (the student) from a pitcher. To assess learning, the teacher then measures the amount of content (curriculum) the student retained, that is, how many beans are in the jar. Assessment is an "event" separate from instruction (Checkley, 1997). In teacher-focused instruction, the curriculum is inert and the student is passive.

Kohn (1993) gives a similar description:

> That theory sees the teacher (or book) as a repository of information that is poured, a little bit at a time, into the empty vessel known as the student. The student's job is to passively retain this information – and now and then, re-gurgitate some of it on command so we can be sure enough of it got in. (p. 213)

In a student-focused classroom, assessment and instruction are interwoven. It is difficult to determine where the teaching ends and assessment begins. The teacher supplies resources such as information, reference materials, organizers, or models. The student selects resources, acts on them, and creates a product. Learning is required to create the product, and creating the product is the learning experience. The student is analogous to a food processor, acting on the ingredients (the curriculum), and thereby personalizing them, creating a unique product (such as a cake) by his or her action. The teacher functions as a mediator between the curriculum and the student, and assesses learning by evaluating the quality of the product. In this sense, the primary activity of the classroom is not the delivery of inert content, but the action of the student with the content.

The primary activity of the classroom is not the delivery of inert content, but the action of the student with the content.

For example, in a teacher-focused classroom the teacher might lecture to students about the steps in a bill becoming a law. Students take notes and are responsible for knowing the steps for an upcoming test. In a student-focused classroom, the teacher and students work together to create the specifics of the curriculum based on student needs and interests (the students choose to write a "candy bill" to allow candy to be eaten in school). The teacher organizes, displays, or coordinates content in the form of resources/raw materials such as information (from textbooks, handouts), reference materials, organizers (steps in writing a bill, steps in how a bill becomes a law), or models (roles in the House of Representatives and U.S. Senate). The student selects resources, develops the content (designs role play, assigns parts), shapes, tailors it to fit his individual needs or interests (the group chooses a "candy bill"). The student organizes, constructs, personalizes the content to have meaning, and transforms the content to create a unique product (writing the bill and the script for the role play). Learning is required to create that product and creating the product is the learning experience. The teacher functions as a mediator between the curriculum and the student, and assesses learning by assessing the quality of the product.

Encouraging student voice in learning activities

The use of the term "voice" in the discussion of classroom learning is both symbolic and literal. Broadly defined, voice indicates the ability of students to have input into such things as classroom rules and procedures, curriculum themes, and methods of learning and assessment. As teachers move toward student-focused instruction, they begin by encouraging student voice in the literal sense. One of the most pervasive indicators of a teacher-focused classroom is the predominance of teacher talk and the control of student talk. Kohn (1993) views the practice as an American tradition:

> One of the most disquieting things about American education is the emphasis placed on being quiet. If we attend to all that is not being said by students, we realize that the absence of children's voices occurs by design and is laboriously enforced. Talking is called 'misbehaving'...Teachers who depart from this norm by letting them talk more freely are said to have lost control of their classrooms (a marvelously revealing phrase). (p.213)

Goodlad (1984) observed that, on average, 70% of class time was teacher talk, most of it telling, not requiring a student response. The chronic problem of teacher talk and student silence has created many passive students at the middle level. The more and the longer teachers talk, the fewer questions students ask, the less confident they are to initiate interaction with the teacher, the less confident they are that what they say matters (Shor, 1992). Many students seem resigned to the pattern, saying in essence, "you're the boss, if you want to do all the talking, we'll just watch."

Obviously, some teacher talk is necessary. Explaining concepts, instructions for assignments, and coaching advice are all justifiable uses of teacher talk. But students need dialogue and social interaction to meet their social needs and to assist in processing information. If the goal is student responsibility for learning, students must be allowed to talk about their learning. The pattern of interaction in the classroom needs to include more dialogue between teachers and students, and more talking to learn. Perhaps a good rule of thumb in planning instruction would be to try to limit teacher talk to no longer than 10 minutes at a time, and no longer than 20 minutes within a class period. This would force the planning of more student-focused activities, more student talk and teacher listening, and more teacher-student dialogue.

Goodlad (1984) observed that, on average, 70% of class time was teacher talk, most of it telling, not requiring a student response.

Teachers can increase student voice in classroom activities by using such methods as the following:

- Use student questions to guide and organize instruction. Ask students to list questions they have about the topic and use them to organize the lesson for the day.

- Encourage students to generate and lead discussions. Student-generated discussions allow students to interact with the content, examine it from various perspectives, and voice their opinions.

- Use dialogue with students to advance the lesson. For example, have students tell the next step in a process, find a deliberate mistake, or give their opinions about a concept just presented.

- Ask thought-provoking questions that force students to use previously learned information to analyze and answer questions.

- Have students summarize the class hour in groups, pairs, or by individually accepting all reactions and opinions.

- Ask for student input into the organization of units, types of assignments, schedules, or classroom problems.

Planning learning around student activities

Student-focused instruction keeps passive methods to a minimum and plans almost all curriculum around student activities. Learning tasks should be designed for active learning and, when possible, include concrete experiences. When 7th and 8th graders were asked to describe their most memorable work in school, students most often cited hands-on science, independent research projects, and stand-up performances such as plays, skits, and speeches.

> Passive learning is not engaging. For students to sense that their work is important, they need to tinker with real world problems, and they need opportunities to construct knowledge. Hard work does not turn students away, but busy-work destroys them. (Wasserstein, 1995)

In other words, students find projects more meaningful not because they are easier, but because they are more challenging:

> Again and again, students equated hard work with success and satisfaction. Moreover, they suggested that challenge is the essence of engagement; when students feel they are doing important work, they are more likely to buy in than not...It is not the instant success but the challenge and victory that give students a sense of power.
> (Wasserstein, 1995, p. 41)

When it is necessary to use direct instruction, time should be a critical factor:

> Cut the length of focused attention time expected or required. Remember that the human brain is poor at non-stop attention. As a guideline, use 5-7 minutes of direct instruction for K-2, 8-12 minutes for grades 3-7, and 12-15 minutes for grades 8-12. After learning, the brain needs time for processing and rest. In a typical classroom, this means rotating mini-lectures, group work, reflection, individual work, and team project time.
> (Jensen, 1998, pp.48-49)

Efforts should be made to relate new information to something students already know or have experienced. Analogies are useful as well as patterns, schemas, and guidelines that help students organize information. Whenever possible, techniques such as inquiry learning,

Socratic questioning, cooperative learning, or investigative research are more active, and preferable to direct instruction or seatwork. Projects that use the arts are especially appropriate as they allow for creativity and personal expression and allow students to communicate their identities in a unique manner.

Projects that use the arts are especially appropriate as they allow for creativity and personal expression and allow students to communicate their identities in a unique manner.

Ideally, students should have some opportunities to engage in individualized goal-setting for academic and behavioral improvement. "Goal-setting should take into account both the interests and concerns of students and the expectations of society" (Vars, 1997, p. 45). Students may set goals for improvement in a specific subject or skill and develop a plan to reach the goal. Goal-setting may also be used by students to design self-initiated research where they investigate a problem of their choice that relates to the curriculum.

Ideal characteristics of student activities are summarized in Figure 2.

Figure 2

Ideal Characteristics of Instructional Activities

- student choice

- student autonomy

- integrates more than one subject

- requires application of skills/content

- allows for a "personal signature"

- culminates in a product that is presented or displayed

(Vatterott, 1995)

Student choice. Students should have more than one choice in how and what they learn, to select the complexity or type of project they do. Open-ended projects are ideal because they allow students to work at different skill levels, and require them to plan, organize, and implement their work (Turner & Meyer, 1995). For instance, students may choose which climate zone to report on (polar, temperate or tropical), which aspect of Chinese culture to research (Confucianism, changing role of women, history of Chinese communism), or which poem to read. Students may choose a question they would like to answer that relates to a topic just studied and identify sources of information to guide their research. In this case, all students learn the same general concepts about climate zones or Chinese culture, but they do so by focusing on a specific area that is of interest to them. By allowing students to reach the same goal through different learning experiences and on different schedules, not all students will create the same product, but they should be able to reach the same goal.

Student autonomy. Students should have some freedom in the way they learn. For instance, a student may have the freedom to read, listen to a tape or lecture, or watch a video to learn information. During a written assignment, students may elect to work at a desk, a table, to sit on the floor, or to work standing by a bookshelf. During a group assignment, students may have a choice of working within a large group, with one person, or working alone. In general, students should have freedom to move about and interact with others in the learning process whenever possible.

Turner and Meyer (1995) suggested that the following questions can serve as barometers of how thoroughly students control their instruction and learning:

1. Are students required to negotiate the level of difficulty?
2. May students adapt the requirements to fit their needs and interests?
3. Do students share in the evaluation process? (p. 23)

Integration of content. Curricular content should be organized around relevant themes with clusters of interdisciplinary concepts, rather than a subject-based, sequential lists of factual information. For instance, when 6th graders at Willard South Elementary in Willard, Missouri, studied ancient Egyptian civilization, they practiced basic math skills using Egyptian numerals, researched the culture, read mystery books with mummies as the central characters, and mummified chickens with oil and spices to demonstrate the embalming process. Beane (1993) has suggested the intersection of students' personal and social concerns such as identities, transitions, and social structures are especially useful in organizing themes. When middle school students were allowed to choose their own themes for an interdisciplinary citizenship education project, they chose such topics as school violence, homelessness, handicapped awareness, and animal rights (Citizenship Education Clearinghouse, 1993).

Application of skills. Too often students are asked to fill in the missing blank, answer the questions at the end of the chapter, or memorize lists of characteristics. The limited value of such activities is described by Kohn (1993):

> We break ideas down into tiny pieces that bear no relation to the whole. We give students a brick of information, followed by another brick, followed by another brick, followed by another brick, until they are graduated, at which point we assume they have a house. What they have is a pile of bricks, and they don't have it for long. (p. 216)

Transmission of low-level factual content should be deemphasized in favor of broad conceptual knowledge and skills that enable students to think critically and creatively and solve problems (O'Neil, 1990). Many teachers encourage the application of skills through the use of problem-based learning.

Problem-based learning uses a real world problem as a starting point for an in-depth investigation of core content. Students take on the real-life roles of scientists, historians, or archaeologists. Problems are ill-structured so that the student must use the inquiry process and reasoning (Checkley, 1997). Problems may be real or fictional, like creating a plan to help an athlete train for the Olympics, designing a program to reduce vandalism in the community, or determining the cause of a polluted lake.

For instance, instead of having students memorize the types of governments and climate zones and their characteristics, students at Parkway Central Middle School in Chesterfield, Missouri, designed their own country, complete with type of government, climate zone and terrain. They determined what industry it would support, compiled laws, and with the help of a computerized program in music, wrote a national anthem.

Allowing for a "personal signature." Just as signatures are unique, assignments that allow for a personal signature give students freedom to make a project unique, unlike anyone else's. The following activities allow students that freedom.

- Write a letter to a new immigrant explaining his/her basic rights as guaranteed by the U.S. Constitution. Use real life examples to illustrate each right.

- Write a story or newspaper article demonstrating your understanding of the 15 vocabulary words for the week.

- Make up a jeopardy game that covers the list of main ideas at the end of the chapter.

- Produce a model of a human cell with household items that approximate the shapes and proportions of the parts.

- Design an experiment to test a simple scientific principle discussed in class.

These assignments allowed students to put their own personal touches and resulted in 20 different "variations on a theme."

"Writing To Learn" instruction typifies this concept when students are allowed to write about things that are meaningful to them. In one special education class at Osage Beach Middle School in Lake Ozark, Missouri, seventh graders collaborated to create a Christmas story titled "The Christmas Santa Was Arrested." The students dictated the story to the teacher who helped them correct grammar and sentence structure as she wrote the story on the board. Students checked the dictionary for spelling, copied the story, designed a cover, and later read the story to a fourth grade class (Vatterott, 1995).

Evaluating student activities

The way learning is assessed determines what will be learned and how it will be learned. According to James McMillan, an education professor at Virginia Commonwealth University, students learn "the real standard" by how an assessment instrument is designed, "If it's a multiple-choice test that requires mostly recall knowledge," then students conclude that the ability to remember facts is important (in Checkley, 1997).

In other words, when designing assessments, teachers, in effect, define the curriculum. What is tested is a reflection of what is valued in learning. Student-focused assessment goes beyond low-level learning and seeks to evaluate broad conceptual learning and higher order objectives.

Before designing assessments, teachers should think carefully about how past grading practices have influenced student motivation. In *Punished by Rewards: The Trouble with Gold Stars, Incentive Plans, A's, Praise, and Other Bribes*, Kohn (1993) offers considerable evidence that an overemphasis on grades negatively influences motivation and performance. For instance, the more concerned students are about the grade they will receive for a task, the less they seem to focus on the task itself, and the less interesting the task becomes. Traditional ABCDF grading also embodies a sorting and ranking system that interferes with the motivation and learning of a significant number of students (Canady, 1989). In a sense, students are separated into learners (A,B, and maybe C students) and losers (D and F students), and when the losers are convinced they cannot be learners, they give up.

Canady (1993) contrasts how assessment in a system concerned about learning will differ from assessment in the traditional sorting and ranking system:

- Work is graded only after non-academic standards, such as neatness and form have been addressed.
- Assignments of unacceptable quality are returned without a grade.
- Assignments may be rewritten to improve the grade.
- Teachers use formative feedback; summative grading.
- The goal of a test is to encourage students to study and organize their notes, not just to memorize key facts.
- Teachers take pride in the number of students who master the content, not the ability of a test to discriminate.

Designing assessments

Assessments that allow students to perform or receive attention, to compete with peers, or to express themselves or their opinions are especially popular with middle level students. The best assessments require students to think and manipulate information in meaningful ways (Combs, 1997). The best assessments encourage mastery learning, allowing all students to achieve some measure of success. This should be possible if assessments are designed to accommodate individual differences in learning style and speed and if students are allowed to express themselves through their preferred modality (Combs, 1997). When possible, assessments should be performance-based, requiring students to show what they have learned in one of three ways: producing knowledge or discourse, creating products or performances, or providing personal reflections. Producing knowledge or discourse might include compiling reports, engaging in a debate, or discussing what they have learned. Personal reflections about what has been learned are often shown in student journals, dictated on cassette tapes, or illustrated through artwork depicting learning. Products or performances might include models or displays, exhibitions or performances for younger groups of students. Figure 3 (p. 58) describes six generic project "templates" used for planning individual or group projects.

When paper and pencil tests must be used, students should know in advance what the test will cover, be allowed to use books or notes as resources (even if only for a portion of the test time), and be given as much time as they need to finish the test. Students can be given choices such as essay or multiple choice versions of the same test, or be allowed to take exams orally. Requirements for performance assessments should be clear to students in advance, with grading rubrics or products of acceptable quality made available as samples.

Creating a rubric to assess student products requires teachers to think through "what counts," what makes a quality product.

> A rubric is a scoring tool that lists the criteria for a piece of work, or 'what counts' (for example, purpose, organization, details, voice, and mechanics are often what count in a piece of writing); it also articulates gradations of quality for each criterion, from excellent to poor. (Goodrich, 1996, p. 14)

Typically a rubric lists criteria for the product on the left, with descriptions of levels of quality across for each criteria. Figure 4 (p. 59) shows an example of a rubric. Rubrics are a preferred method of project evaluation for several reasons:

> ...they help define 'quality'...they help students become more thoughtful judges of the quality of their own and others work...[and] they reduce the amount of time teachers spend evaluating student work. (Goodrich, 1996)

Figure 3

Six Templates for Individual or Group Projects

1. **Talk show script/enactment**
    Identify a theme for the show, compose the script, list of guests, and interviews, and present to the class.
    EXAMPLES: Interview characters from *To Kill a Mockingbird*.
    Interview important people from a period of history.

2. **Board game**
    Create a board game that shows the steps in a process, or progression of a series of events.
    EXAMPLES: The path of food through the digestive system.
    What leads to a war?
    Steps in solving a mathematical or scientific problem.

3. **Role play**
    Create roles and dialogue for characters to illustrate a process or show an analogy of a relationship.
    EXAMPLES: How a bill becomes a law (with senators, representatives, the bill).
    How blood carries oxygen through the body (train and train stations).

4. **Models**
    EXAMPLES: Use math concepts to build a doll house, determine how much flooring, wallpaper to buy.
    Build a model showing what causes a flood.

5. **Mini-museum or museum display**
    Make a display with descriptive signs that illustrates a process or concept or synthesizes information about a concept.
    EXAMPLES: A display describing the various forms of rocks.
    A display depicting the significant events during a specific presidency.

6. **Small business**
    Create a small business in which you make and market a product or service. Costs and overhead must be computed and the business must be able to make a profit. Apply math and economics concepts learned in class.
    EXAMPLES: Paper cups decorated and filled with popcorn.
    Note delivery service.
    Custom music tape service (recording favorite songs on cassette tape).

Figure 4

Sample Rubric for an Invention Report

CRITERIA	QUALITY		
Did I get my audience's attention?	Creative beginning	Boring beginning	No beginning
Did I tell what kind of book?	Tells exactly what type of book it is	Not sure, not clear	Didn't mention it
Did I tell something about the main character?	Included facts about character	Slid over character	Did not tell anything about main character
Did I mention the setting?	Tells when and where story takes place	Not sure, not clear	Didn't mention setting
Did I tell one interesting part?	Made it sound interesting – I want to buy it!	Told part and skipped on to something else	Forgot to do it
Did I tell who might like the book?	Did tell	Skipped over it	Forgot to do it
How did I look?	Hair combed, neat, clean clothes, smiled, looked up, happy	Lazy look	Just-got-out-of-bed look, head down
How did I sound?	Clear, strong, cheerful voice.	No expression in voice	Difficult to understand – 6-inch voice or screeching

(Goodrich, 1996, p. 15)

When properly designed, portfolios are another useful tool for evaluating student work. A portfolio is a planned collection of student work that shows progress or growth. "This collection must include student participation in selection of portfolio content, the guidelines for selection, the criteria for judging merit, and evidence of student self-reflection" (Higgins and Heglie-King, 1997, p. 23). Portfolios provide opportunities for students to plan and organize their work, self-evaluate using standards, document progress in learning, and communicate about their learning through the portfolio. Standards of quality must be clearly outlined, however, to prevent products which "show well" but hide a shallow grasp of the content. Teachers must guard against weighing appearance and presentation more heavily than content or learning progress. (For more about assessments, see *Middle School Journal, Volume 25* [2], and *Educational Leadership,* Volume *52* [2]).

Student portfolios are most useful when used by the students to plan, organize, and lead their own parent conferences.

Student portfolios are most useful when they are used by the students to plan, organize, and lead their own parent conferences. Student-led conferences allow students to self-evaluate progress, identify their strengths and weaknesses, and set goals. At Sherwood Elementary School in Arnold, Missouri, students conduct their own parent conferences and develop Personal Growth Plans which they discuss during the conference. The Personal Growth Plan is designed collaboratively by a student and his/her teacher to reflect competencies the student has not yet mastered and areas that may be affecting academic performance (see Figure 5, p. 61, for a sample Personal Growth Plan).

Redirecting time and energy

Because teachers never have enough time or energy to accomplish what they want, they often resort to practices which they believe are expedient. Concerned about time, teachers resort to lecturing, not allowing their students to discover information. In some classrooms, teachers answer their own questions without waiting for their students to think, not allowing them a moment to make their own meaning. It seems more efficient to do it for them, and in the process students learn how not to learn, how to wait and not have to answer, and how to avoid having to think. Learning often gets short-circuited by an obsession to time on task, regardless of the learning value of the task. In reality, meaningful learning is messy and time-consuming.

Figure 5

Sample Sixth Grade Student Growth Plan

I am very happy that I improved on two things that were recommended in my last growth plan, which were, grammar and playing better during gym. Now I have three other things I am working on for the last term. These are to try to concentrate on my work, trying not to laugh so much in class, and improve my test marks in science and social studies tests.

I am satisfied that I made a good progress in grammar, but I am also happy that I improved in physical education class. I can finally bump and serve a volleyball. I may not be such a good basketball player, but I know how to control a ball.

This term I want to improve on every science and social studies test I take. I will also try harder not to laugh so much in class. I always have a bit of trouble doing science and social studies tests. I sometimes take too long thinking on one question. Laughing in class is the worst. Once I start laughing I cannot stop myself. I hope I can succeed in these things for next term.

How I am going to improve is not a problem. I have just got to work harder! When I know there is a science or social studies test coming up, I will start studying right away. I will also try to remember the important things Mr. Brown had said during class discussions. When I am doing my work, I will try to avoid the funny things my friends say. That is all I can think of to improve.

(from Sherwood Elementary School, Arnold, Missouri)

Teachers will often say that designing an active lesson is more time consuming than planning a lecture. In the traditional teach and test system, information is typically presented one time, one way, students do some sort of assignment to reinforce or practice, and then they are tested. Teachers then grade and assign a label (ABCDF) to students' work and they are finished. This seems fast and allows them to "cover" more content. It may be efficient in terms of amount covered, but possibly not efficient in the amount learned.

In student-focused instruction, teacher time and energy is directed away from content presentation and grading papers and into the development of meaningful activities and assessments. Several steps teachers might go through in the process of planning student activities are listed below:

1. **Structuring the activity:** The teacher begins by determining objectives for the activity, the pattern of instruction (group instruction, then the learning task, then the follow-up or in-depth activities), and a preliminary time schedule.

2. **Determining a method for evaluation:** The teacher may create a rubric that includes criteria and rankings of quality for each of the criteria. Students may be asked to help create the rubric or offer suggestions for how the activity will be evaluated.

3. **Assembling resources or reference materials necessary for the student to complete the activity:** Collecting references such as textbooks, newspapers or news magazines, and materials such as construction paper, glue, tape, markers, or scissors.

4. **Setting up learning centers:** Learning centers could include computers to access information, equipment to do experiments, or simply designated spaces to spread out the reference material to avoid student congestion. Assigning areas for group work or for construction of games may also be helpful.

5. **Teaching the skills necessary to complete the task:** This could include the proper form for a personal letter, how to write a persuasive essay, or modeling a procedure.

6. **Monitoring students during their work on the task:** This would be done on a daily basis, preferably with a visible timeline for completing each stage of the unit (Vatterott, 1995).

In reality, planning student-focused instruction should require no more teacher time and energy than planning traditional teacher-focused instruction. In student-focused instruction, as students take more responsibility for their own learning, teachers spend less time lecturing, less time struggling to motivate students, and more time structuring and individualizing learning experiences.

Conclusion

Tackling student-focused curriculum and instruction is a big job. Teachers can begin by involving students in their curriculum planning. They can give students choices about learning. They can provide opportunities for middle school students to define themselves, become part of a group, and to feel like competent learners. Student-focused instruction can help meet students' developmental needs and improve their motivation to learn. ■

Special thanks to Kerry Kew, Oakville Junior High School, and Steve Toomey, Lindbergh High School, both in St. Louis, Missouri, for many of the examples of student-focused instruction I observed in their classrooms and have shared in this chapter.

V

Empowering Programs

This last chapter provides a sampling of the types of programs that can help empower young adolescents. They are broadly grouped into remediation, curriculum, programs to monitor progress, school membership, co-curricular, behavioral success, community service, and student governance. A brief description of the idea or program is followed by a source to contact for additional information. After each section are references for useful Internet sites that will provide further information on the topic.

Remediation and Support

1. Saturday School

Using a grant written under Title I, Pattonville Heights Middle School operates a Saturday School Program for students who choose to participate in a self-help program. Student work is generated by the student's regular classroom teachers and may be work that has been missed, needs to be redone, or work that the student needs extra help to complete. Saturday School is not a replacement for regular weekday class instruction. Students are not allowed to attend Saturday School if they waste class time during the previous week. A mid-morning brunch prepared by school administrators and volunteers has become a great time for visiting with the students and validating their wise decision to take some control and responsibility for their success in school.

CONTACT
Karen Mayberry
Pattonville Heights Middle School
195 Fee Fee Road
Maryland Heights, MO 63043
(314) 213-8306

2. Accelerating At-Risk Eighth Graders

Normandy Junior High School offers unique opportunities for students who are behind academically and overage for their grade. Some of the students have already been retained twice in elementary school and want most to be with students their own age. Called a "transition program," the program is available for eighth graders (aged 15 by January 30) who maintain a "C" average during the first semester of the 8th grade. Students who qualify take some 8th grade classes and some 9th grade classes during their second semester of the 8th grade. They complete their 9th grade classes in summer school and in the fall enter high school as 10th graders. They are all placed in the same 8th grade team and receive special advising.

CONTACT:
> Normandy Junior High School
> 7855 Natural Bridge Road
> St. Louis, MO 63121-4696
> (314) 389-8005

3. Intensive Core Curriculum (ICC)

Rolla Junior High School offers a similar program of intensive study for students who have been retained at some point in their academic careers. Students take classes in the four academic areas in 80 minute blocks combining 8th and 9th grade curriculum. They receive one elective credit, which is a combination of physical education, careers, and computers. They leave the junior high school as prepared as every other 9th grader for the 10th grade. They will earn a total of five credits out of a possible seven.

CONTACT:
> Dr. Steve Laub
> Rolla Junior High School
> 1360 Soest Road
> Rolla, MO 65401
> (573) 364-3014

4. Stand By Me After-School Tutoring

This program at Kirksville Middle School is a holistic intervention to help at-risk students. Students receive after-school tutoring three days a week. No more than five students work with a single teacher in a long-term tutoring/mentoring relationship. The coordinator has a degree in social work and experience working with social service programs serving at-risk families. The coordinator helps the families communicate positively with the school and helps with such basic needs as shelter, heat/utilities, medical care, and employment by connecting the families with appropriate resources.

CONTACT:
    Kirksville Middle School
    1515 Cottage Grove
    Kirksville, MO 63501-3979
    (660) 665-3793

5. Internet Sites

http://www.arjuvjust.org/news.html

This site includes remediation programs and services funded by the Arkansas Coalition for Juvenile Justice and Delinquency Prevention. Programs include:

a)   Schooling for suspended or expelled students in El Dorado.

    CONTACT: Cynthia Baston
    General e-mail account: acjj@arjuvjust.org

b)   Parenting and Self-Esteem building for 5th and 6th graders in Hope, Arkansas.

    CONTACT: Kenneth Muldrew
    General e-mail: acjj@arjuvjust.org

http://www.naesp.org/atrisk2.htm

This National Association of Elementary School Principals' site targets at-risk students. There are some references to younger grades, but it also addresses sixth and seventh grade students. Some of the programs included at this site are:

a)   Friday's Kids: This program gives extra assistance to students by having them meet once a week with a special services teacher to work on areas in which they need additional help.

b)   Back on Track: this program is designed for over-age students going into seventh grade and trying to get on track again with peers. The staff selects students to take the core classes in their last year of middle school, and they are transported at different times during the year to the high school for elective courses. It provides an accelerated program so students can complete middle school and enter the ninth grade by passing one year at the middle school.

c)   A Sense of Belonging: This program involves students in the educational community. For example, students are trained to become conflict managers and student buddies for younger grades. These kids all have regular jobs on campus (Safety Patrol Officer, Principal's Assistant).

CONTACT: General e-mail: naesp@naesp.org

Innovative Curriculum

1. Citizenship Education Clearing House

Citizenship Education Clearing House (CECH, pronounced "check") has conducted programs in civic education since the 1960s. CECH's programs give middle and high school students a real-life experience in the political process, with the expectation that "learning the system" will encourage them to participate in politics when they become adults. For instance, in Local Government CECH-UP, middle school students study local government in the St. Louis area, meet with local officials, travel to the sites of local government activities, and develop projects in their own communities. High school students study major state issues in day-long seminars at UM-St. Louis and travel to the state capital for discussions with legislators.

CONTACT:
Timothy G. O'Rourke
Teresa M. Fischer Professor of Citizenship Education
School of Education, UM-St. Louis
357 Marillac Hall
St. Louis, MO 63121
(314) 516-6853
e-mail TG_OROURKE@UMSL.EDU

2. Reading Across Disciplines

RAD (Reading Across Disciplines) is a reading and study skills program at Hollenbeck Middle School. Skills taught include previewing a reading assignment, double column note taking, time management, summarizing, and test taking. One team teacher introduces, teaches, and models the skill. The other team teachers reinforce the skills in their classes, using common terminology and techniques. A scope and sequence developed for the year determines when and which teacher introduces a particular skill. Pre- and post-testing have shown consistent gains in vocabulary and comprehension.

CONTACT:
> Gary Lacey
> Hollenbeck Middle School
> 4555 Central School Road
> St. Charles, MO 63304
> (314) 441-1501

3. Eighth Grade Special Interest Electives

At Wentzville Middle School, to alleviate overcrowding in the traditional electives, eighth graders are allowed to sign up for one semester electives taught by academic teachers. The courses have shown students the relevance of academics to real life and have been a fun way to reinforce basic skills. Some of the more popular courses have been History of Film, Creative Writing, Ecology, and Cultures.

CONTACT:
> Susan Bell
> Wentzville South Middle School
> 561 East Highway N
> Wentzville, MO 63385
> (314) 327-3928

4. Internet Sites

HYPERLINK http://www.des-moines.k12.ia.us/ http://www.des-moines.k12.ia.us/Middle_Schools/Goodrell/projects.htm

The "Baby Think it Over" project in the seventh grade Family Living Course, provides infant simulators to its students. They take the simulator home over the weekend and write about their experiences.

The baby is programmed to cry at irregular intervals, lasting between 5 and 30 minutes. The dolls are about 20 inches long and weigh 7 to 8 pounds. It is sponsored by the Roy J. Carver Charitable Trust. The project head is Laura Anspach.

CONTACT: HYPERLINK mailto:goodrell-ms@dmps.des-moines.k12.ia.us goodrell-ms@dmps.des-moines.k12.ia.us

http://www.pathfinder.com/corp/turner/turnerpr/tcm0602.html

TCM BY THE BOOK is an effort to improve reading. It uses pre-recorded classic movies with curricular materials to help students in language arts or across several disciplines. Some of the books taught are *Ivanhoe, Little Women,* and *The Red Badge of Courage.* It was introduced by Turner Broadcasting in September of 1997.

CONTACT: http://learning.turner.com

http://www.education-world.com/

In the Free Volunteer Reading (FVR) program there are almost no guidelines as to what the students read. Whether they report on it in class or whether they read at home, it is sustained silent reading in a very pure form. The school sets aside a 45-minute period when the students spend the first 30-35 minutes reading and then the next ten talking about the book they are reading, but the talk is totally voluntary. There are motivators for doing the reading, particular Club Levels; 200 page Club, 300 page Club. There are monitoring systems for students who are poor readers too. There are links here to sites that talk more about this particular program.

CONTACT: HYPERLINK http://www.education-world.com/contact http://www.education-world.com/contact

http://darwin.cshl.org/middle.html

This innovative curricular idea takes students to a teaching laboratory at the DNA Learning Center where students are exposed to Genetics and Human Genetics experiences. The program allows students hands-on time to develop creative and critical thinking skills. An example of a few of the labs include: Variability and Inheritance – Fruit

Fly Experiment; DNA Structure and Recombination – Model Building or how cells recombine; Corn Genetics and Mendelian Inheritance – Punnett Squares

> CONTACT: Ms. Judy Cumella (516) 367-7240
> Email: dnalc@cshl.org

Programs for Monitoring and Reporting Student Progress

1. Personal Acceptance and Learning Support (PALS)

PALS is a special support program for at-risk students at Fort Zumwalt South Middle School. Students referred to PALS receive guidance in developing and applying study skills, specific team interventions, and close monitoring by the counselor. Each student in this group is as-signed a staff member who acts as a mentor and participates in special activities with them. Students receive biweekly progress reports, extra time with counselors, and expanded educational opportunities such as guest speakers and field trips throughout the year.

CONTACT:
> Ft. Zumwalt South Middle School
> 300 Knaust Road
> St. Peters, MO 63376-1796
> (314) 272-6620

2. Student-Led Parent Conferences

Students at Sherwood Elementary School assume an active role in planning, implementing, conducting, and evaluating parent conferences. Students work collaboratively with their teachers to develop a Personal Growth Plan identifying areas where the students have not achieved mastery, or areas of personal growth most affecting performance. Stu-dents select papers from their portfolios to present, review, and discuss at their parent conference. Students lead their own conferences based on their portfolios and their knowledge of their strengths and weak-nesses. Students come to the conference with "two stars and a wish," two things they are proud of, and one thing they would like to improve.

CONTACT:
>Mike Allison
>Sherwood Elementary School
>1769 Missouri State Road
>Arnold, MO 63010
>(314) 296-1413

3. Narrative Report Cards

Each academic team at Lewis and Clark Middle School designs its own narrative report card, approved by the principal. The quarterly report cards list course outcomes, work habits, narrative comments, and an overall rating for the student's work in that subject. The narratives provide parents with specific feedback on their child's progress.

CONTACT:
>Dr. Bob Steffes
>Lewis and Clark Middle School
>325 Lewis and Clark Drive
>Jefferson City, MO 65101
>(573) 659-3200

School Membership and Identity Programs

1.   Making It Happen

The original target audience for this program consisted of African American students who lived in the city but attended suburban Wydown Middle School as part of a voluntary desegregation program. The program is now open to all students. The focus of the program is to enhance academic achievement through a feeling of membership. The student is matched with a mentor who works with the student and parent. Students, mentors, and parents participate in a wide variety of educational and recreational experiences together. The program also provides tutoring once a week (using area college students as tutors) and parent education to assist parents in helping students succeed academically.

CONTACT:
>Tyrone McNichols
>Wydown Middle School
>6500 Wydown Blvd.
>Clayton, MO 63105
>(314)726-5222

2. Youth Night

Youth Night is a once-a-month lock-in program planned and implemented by a local advisory board comprised of Division of Family Services, Jefferson City Housing Authority, and Jefferson City Public School representatives. Local law enforcement agencies, Juvenile Court, YMCA, and other community groups volunteer time and resources to provide the lock-in free of charge. The lock-ins are held at Thomas Jefferson Middle School during the school year and at the YMCA during June, July, and August. Approximately 300 youths participate in each 7 P.M. to 7 A.M. lock-in. Each monthly lock-in surrounds a theme such as drugs, alcohol, violence, or gangs. Educational programming is presented on each monthly issue by a local hospital or other community professionals. Food, music, and recreational activities are provided.

CONTACT:
> Fern Ward
> Thomas Jefferson Middle School
> 1201 Fairgrounds Road
> Jefferson City, MO 65109
> (573) 659-3250

Co-curricular Programs

1. CALM Program

The CALM program is designed to help African American males develop skills needed to achieve academically, socially, and emotionally. All 6th grade black males and new 7th and 8th grade black males are invited to join this three-year program. During the first year, students develop personal action plans and are exposed to films, books, and articles that depict leadership qualities exhibited by African American males. During the second year, students visit successful African American males in the community. During the third year, students complete 30 hours of community service and are matched with a Clayton High School student (from the high school they will attend) who provides support and guidance for the transition to the high school.

CONTACT:
> Tyrone McNichols
> Wydown Middle School
> 6500 Wydown Blvd.
> Clayton, Missouri 63105
> (314) 726-5222

2. The Stream Team

The Stream Team is part of an adopt-a-stream program sponsored by the Missouri Department of Conservation and Natural Resources. At Hollenbeck Middle School it operates as an after-school club. Teams of students from around the school district have adopted a creek that crosses district property. They assume responsibility for clean up and monitoring activities of the stream. The program allows students to use environmental and ecological concepts learned in their science classes through hands-on activities. It also provides students with a connection to state government, and gives them a chance to perform a service to the community.

CONTACT:
> Hollenbeck Middle School
> 4555 Central School Road
> St. Charles, MO 63304
> (314) 441-1501

3. Healthy Alternative for Relationships among Teens (HART)

The Project HART curriculum was originally developed by the Women's Self-Help Center and the Progressive Youth Center in St. Louis. The staff at Nipher Middle School worked with their representatives to adapt their materials for presenting the basic skills of safe and non-violent relationships to students in grades 6-8. Students at all levels participate in workshops on Anger Management, Communication, Challenging Sexual Harassment, and Gender Equity. Creating Safe Relationships is presented to the eighth grade only.

CONTACT:
> Sheri Peyton
> Nipher Middle School
> 700 South Kirkwood Road
> Kirkwood, MO 63122
> (314) 966-9936

4. Positive Attitudes Leading to Success (PALS)

The PALS program is a partnership between Lewis and Clark Middle School and two local elementary schools. LCMS students travel to each elementary school one day each week for two hours to serve as tutors and classroom assistants. These students work one-on-one with selected students and/or assist with entire classrooms of students. Since students need to serve as positive role models, participating students must meet strict criteria in the areas of academics and behavior. The program is designed to create positive opportunities for students considered to be at-risk in the participating schools.

CONTACT:
> Dr. Bob Steffes
> Lewis and Clark Middle School
> 325 Lewis and Clark Drive
> Jefferson City, MO 65101
> (573) 659-3200

5. Internet Sites

http://www.des-moines.k12.ia.us/Middle_School/Goodrell/projects.htm

This school is working in cooperation with the Roy J. Carver Charitable Trust to build a Nature Center at the school. The students have built several different habitats (prairies, woodlands, and ponds) to display their different look and function. The students are developing portfolios and journals along with a photographic record of what is being done.

> CONTACT: goodrell-ms@mps.des-moines.k12.ia.us

http://www.wh-gardnerms.bucksport.k12.me.us/cocur~1.html

Bucksport Middle School believes that everyone should have a chance to participate in co-curricular activities. They have made an effort to provide both interscholastic and intramural activities for students during all sports seasons. These programs are offered at a variety of skill levels for students so they may participate at a comfortable level. The clubs and organizations that the school also sponsors include S.H.A.R.P. (Students Helping Alcohol-Related Problems), and Teen Theater.

> CONTACT: flisnik@saturn.caps.maine.edu

Behavior Improvement Programs

1. Operation Teamwork

The purpose of this program at Sperreng Middle School is to reward students for resolving conflicts through peer mediation rather than fights. Teams receive points for having no fights, no office referrals, and no suspensions. Teams compete against their own grade level for short-term prizes awarded at the end of each month and long-term prizes awarded at the end of the year. Teachers keep score, and weekly updates are given in the morning announcements. Each team is given an Operation Teamwork banner, which is removed if there is a fight.

CONTACT:
> David Kew
> Robert H. Sperreng Middle School
> 12111 Tesson Ferry
> St. Louis, MO 63128
> (314) 729-2420

2. Winning Friendships

The National Council on Alcoholism and Drug Abuse-St. Louis Area offers a conflict resolution program for students in kindergarten through grade six. The program is offered one hour a week for five weeks and covers topics such as hurtful language, teamwork, "you cannot not communicate!", "'stuffing' feelings can be hazardous to your health," and five steps to peaceful problem solving.

CONTACT:
> Connie Otto
> National Council on Alcoholism and Drug Abuse-St. Louis Area
> 8790 Manchester Road
> St. Louis, MO 63144
> (314) 962-3456

3. Positive Alternative to Suspension (PAS)

The Fort Zumwalt School District offers PAS as an optional program to assist students assigned to long-term suspension. The goal of PAS is to help students return to their home school without current conflict. PAS students continue their academic work using the PLATO learning system (a computer based academic program). They receive Aggression Replacement Training and individualized assistance as needed. Parent and family participation in weekly meetings is an integral part of the program.

CONTACT:
> Beth Niedergerke
> PAS
> Ft. Zumwalt School District Annex
> 203 Church Street
> O'Fallon, MO 63366
> (314) 272-6620

4. Alternative Discipline Center

Parkway School District offers an Alternative Discipline Center as a second chance for students who have been suspended for longer than 10 days. Students may choose to attend the Alternative Discipline Center for the last 10 days of their suspension. Regardless of the offense, the ADC staff believes that each student "deserves the opportunity to maintain his academic standing while serving his suspension, and to regain the favorable regard of his school." The staff helps students keep up with academic work and formally assesses math, reading, and study skills. In a supportive and uncritical environment, the staff encourages students to recognize their own talents and accept their limitations. The staff also facilitates a social skills program and encourages students to set goals while at the center and for their return to school. A variety of student services personnel are also available to assist ADC staff on an as-needed basis.

CONTACT:
> Jody Stauffer
> Coordinator of Student Development
> Parkway School District
> 455 N. Woods Mill Road
> Chesterfield, MO 63017
> (314) 415-6931

5. Internet Sites

http://www.co.washington.or.us/sheriff/service/school_p.htm

This is a pilot program that was implemented in several different middle schools (Mt. View, Highland Park, Neil Armstrong, and Tom McCall). It offers conflict resolution, positive problem solving, substance abuse and gang resistance, and good citizenship skill instruction to students to become Student Safety Officers. They function as mediators to resolve conflicts. As a result of the program, suspensions and expulsions for safety related issues were reduced 20%. Feedback has reported a huge improvement in student behavior.

> CONTACT: Sheriff's Office E-mail:
> sheriff.webmaster@co.washington.or.us

HYPERLINK http://www.oseda.missouri.edu/kidcnt/reports/ http://www.oseda.missouri.edu/kidcnt/reports/teenpreg/tn2tn.html

InterACT Teen-to-Teen Theater is a company of high school and middle school students who develop and perform short plays dealing with teen issues that include peer pressure, pregnancy, and violence. The students' plays have unresolved conclusions which give the audience a chance to participate and resolve the issue at hand. The target groups are for 13-19 year old students but the program lends itself well to a middle school population. It teaches responsible alternatives to sometimes irresponsible actions.

CONTACT:
> Rick J. Pummer, Ph.D.
> Planned Parenthood of Central Missouri
> 711 North Providence Road
> Columbia, MO 65203

http://www.cbaa.org/topten.htm

Lockland Middle School in Tennessee has a "Set A Good Example Club." The students in the club are encouraged to increase individual and school pride by improving the environment and behavior, and displaying positive attitudes. They sign a contract upon joining the club that states they will not bring guns or illegal drugs to school. They also must work on a service project that benefits the school and the community. This particular program won national recognition and awards from the CBAA. It would be a good program to implement as both a behavior improvement and a community service program.

CONTACT
  CBAA
  13428 Macella Avenue, Suite 248
  Marina del Ray, CA 90292
  (310) 821-8073

Community Service Programs

1. Food for the Homeless Shelter

After completing a unit about homelessness, students at Nipher Middle School initiated a service project to provide sandwiches for a local homeless shelter. The project has continued over the last few years. The students work in partnership with the PTO and a local bakery. Two days each month, stations are set up in the cafeteria during advisory time so that all students have the opportunity to assist in the sandwich preparation. PTO volunteers purchase meat and cheese, sanitary gloves, and wrapping materials. The students provide the work force. Designated students and the service learning coordinator deliver the sandwiches each month. Classroom discussions and writing assignments help students understand what their contributions mean to the community.

CONTACT:
  Janet Schuster, Service Learning Coordinator
  Nipher Middle School
  700 South Kirkwood Road
  Kirkwood, MO 63122
  (314) 965-9580

2. Required Community Service

Holman Middle School provides the opportunity for community service at all grade levels. However, in the 8th grade students are required to complete 15 hours of community service during the year. Students who cannot or do not want to participate are provided an alternate assignment in their social studies class. A staff coordinator works with community agencies and elementary schools to arrange for the students to complete community service. Students who complete community service at Holman or at one of the elementary schools serve as tutors for younger students or provide assistance to the teaching staff. Students also participate in the National Day of Service (Servathon) in April.

CONTACT:
    Dr. John A. Pohl or Ms. Kathleen Oster
    Holman Middle School
    11055 St. Charles Rock Road
    St. Ann, MO 63074
    (314) 213-8032

3. National Helpers Network

The National Helpers Network is a resource that addresses the needs and abilities of young adolescents through community service. They have helped start programs in New York City, 43 states, and 6 foreign countries. The program allows young people to do responsible and important work in their schools and communities through supervised community service which included "homework helpers," day care assistance, oral histories with senior citizens, work at food banks, and many other projects. They provide a resource library, a newsletter, brochures, training tools, and videos for both adolescents and adult trainers.

CONTACT:
    Deidre C. Meyerson, Executive Director
    National Helpers Network, Inc.
    c/o CASE
    25 West 43rd Street, Suite 612
    New York, New York 10036-8099
(This program was featured in *Middle School Journal, 28* [2].)

http://penny.myriad.net/index.html

The Sam Rayburn Middle School in Bryan, Texas, has a program where a class collects pennies to sponsor a guide dog. The students and the cooperating teacher are in charge of raising a dog for the Southwest Guide Dog Foundation. This foundation supplies guide dogs for disabled citizens in the community that would benefit from such an animal. The students work with the dogs until they are about 18 months before going on to more intense guide dog training. There is a list of related sites that you can contact for more information.

    Contact E-mail: HYPERLINK mailto:Penny@myriad.net
    Penny@myriad.net
    http://cust.iamerica.net/swoidgf

http://www.youthresources.org/service/blind.htm

This is a general site that has successful community-oriented programs for schools. One program that not only helps in the community but improves students' reading skills is, "Helping the Blind to Read." Students record selected readings for students who are sightless. They also write, direct, and record original stories for these students.

E-mail: info@youthresources.org

http://newhorizons.org/trm_sl3.html

At Shuksan Middle School in Bellingham, Washington, a sixth grade teacher connects with a fifth grade teacher, creating a partnership. The 6th grade students become penpals with the 5th grade students. They talk about class projects, middle school regulations, and more. They culminate by participating in environmental service projects in the spring, but the communication goes on through the spring as well when the sixth grade hosts a building orientation for the fifth grade students.

http://newhorizons.org

E-mail: building@newhorizons.org

Student Governance Programs

1. Town Councils

The message about student government at Mount View Middle School is that leadership is service, not power. Each grade level has its own town council, with two elected representatives from each advisory class. The town council meets in grade level meetings once or twice a month to discuss proposals, concerns, suggestions, or needs. An adult advisor for each grade level attends the meetings and communicates meeting information to the grade level teams of teachers. The town councils plan and implement social events and community service projects. All students are eligible to participate in the town council. Town Council meetings allow students to voice their opinions and concerns about school issues and practices. Students may also introduce proposals for bills to be voted into law.

CONTACT:
  Beverly Koren
  Mount View Middle School
  12101 Woodford Drive
  Marriottsville, Maryland 21104
  (410) 313-5545

2. Student Leadership Conference

Prior to the student council election process each fall at Sedalia Middle School, students must decide to run for an office in student government. Upon that declaration, they commit to attending a leadership conference organized by the school. All prospective candidates participate in activities that help promote responsible decision making, foster appropriate attitudes about governing, and develop basic human relations skills. Activities are designed to prepare prospective candidates for running for office and eventually serving the student body in a productive manner. Activities focus on such skills as decision making, communication, working effectively in groups, reaching goals, and managing resources.

CONTACT:
  Laura McKay Cooke
  Sedalia Middle School
  2205 South Ingram Avenue
  Sedalia, MO 65301
  (660) 827-3100

3. Microsociety, Inc.

West Middle School in Sioux City has a Microsociety operating in its school. A Constitutional Convention determines the laws and the "Bill of Rights and Responsibilities." A monetary system is devised, businesses established, and a government elected. During the last hour of the day, students "go to work." Students earn "money" and spend it at the various businesses. Student jobs may be anything from reporting news, to running a business (product or service), to being a judge, policeman, or other government employee. Microsociety was the brainchild of teacher George Richmond, who eventually established Microsociety, Inc., as a non-profit organization.

CONTACT:

Pam Coad or Donna Wilson
West Middle School
1211 W. Fifth Street
Sioux City, IA 51103
(712) 279-6813
OR:
Microsociety, Inc.
603 Cherry Street
Suite 200
Philadelphia, PA 19106
(215) 922-4006

4. Internet Sites

http://www.horacemann.org/activities/studgov/index.html

The Horace Mann School in New York City elects its own government, with executive, legislative, and judicial branches to which students are elected. This governing council is the primary legislative branch for the school. The bills are either passed or vetoed by this government. They can hear disciplinary cases from students as well. The Middle School Council has taken over the role of individual grade governments, but this new government has members from all grade levels.

CONTACT: webmaster@horacemann.pvt.k12.ny.us

http://www.mcps,k12.md.us/schools/rica/index.html

SGA representatives (one per room) from Horace Mann are elected in the fall and meet weekly at lunch during the semester. The SGA presidents are partly responsible for level system moves and for distributing certificates for the week's successful students. These successful student awards lead up to a Successful Week Trip, in which students who are doing well for eight of ten days participate in an extracurricular activity. This trip happens once a month and is set up and sponsored by the SGA and the coordinating teacher.

http://www.mcps.k12.md.us/schools/ricsgues.htm ■

REFERENCES

Apple, M. W., & Beane, J. A. (Eds.). (1995). *Democratic Schools.* Alexandria, VA: Association for Supervision and Curriculum Development.

Arhar, J. M. (1992). Interdisciplinary teaming and the social bonding of middle level students. In J. L. Irvin (Ed.), *Transforming middle level education: Perspectives and possibilities* (pp. 139-162). Boston: Allyn and Bacon.

Armstrong, T. (1994). *Multiple intelligences in the classroom.* Alexandria, VA: Association for Supervision and Curriculum Development.

Barth, R. (1990). *Improving schools from within.* San Francisco: Jossey-Bass Incorporated Publishers.

Beane, J. (1993). *A middle school curriculum: From rhetoric to reality.* Columbus, Ohio: National Middle School Association.

Beane, J. (1997). *Curriculum integration: Designing the core of democratic education.* New York: Teachers College Press.

Bonstingl, J. J. (1992). The quality revolution. *Educational Leadership, 50* (3), 4-9.

Brandt, R. (Ed.). (1992). Untracking for Equity [Special Issue]. *Educational Leadership,* 50 (2).

Brandt, R. (Ed.). (1994). Reporting What Students Are Learning [Special Issue]. *Educational Leadership, 52* (2).

Brandt, R. (1992). On building learning communities: A conversation with Hank Levin. *Educational Leadership, 50* (1), 19-23.

Brooks, J. G., & Brooks, M. G. (1993). *In search of understanding: The case for constructivist classrooms.* Alexandria, VA: Association for Supervision and Curriculum Development.

Caine, R. N., & Caine, G. (1991). *Making connections: Teaching and the human brain.* Alexandria, VA: Association for Supervision and Curriculum Development.

Canady, R. L. (1993, March). *Grading practices which decrease the odds for student success.* Paper presented at the ASCD annual conference, Washington, DC.

Canady, R. L., & Hotchkiss, P. R. (1989). It's a good score! Just a bad grade. *Phi Delta Kappan, 71* (1), 68-71.

Carnegie Council on Adolescent Development. (1989). *Turning points: Preparing American youth for the 21st century.* New York: Carnegie Corporation.

Checkley, K. (1997, Summer). Problem-based learning: The search for solutions to life's messy problems. *Association for Supervision and Curriculum Development Curriculum Update,* 1-8.

Citizenship Education Clearinghouse. (1993). Citizenship Education Clearinghouse student presentations, St. Louis, MO.

Combs, D. (1997). Using alternative assessment to provide options for student success. *Middle School Journal, 29* (1), 3-8.

Crary, E. (1990). *Pick up your socks – and other skills growing children need!* Seattle, WA: Parenting Press.

Cusick, P. A. (1989). *The educational system: Its nature and logic.* New York: McGraw-Hill.

Curwin, R. L., & Mendler, A. N. (1997). *As tough as necessary: Countering violence, aggression, and hostility in our schools.* Alexandria, VA: Association for Supervision and Curriculum Development.

DeVries, R., & Kohlberg, L. (1987). *Constructivist early education: Overview and comparison with other programs.* Washington, DC: National Association for the Education of Young Children.

Dickinson, T. (Ed.). (1993). Alternative Assessment Theme Issue. *Middle School Journal, 25* (2).

Dreikurs, R. (1987). *Children: The challenge.* New York: E.P. Dutton.

Dunn, R., & Dunn, K. (1978). *Teaching students through their individual learning styles.* Reston, VA: Reston Publications.

Dunn, R., Beaudry, J. S., & Klavas, A. (1989). Survey of research on learning styles. *Educational Leadership, 46* (6), 50-52.

Dweck, C. (1992, February). Performance vs. Learning. Presented at meeting of Missouri Association for Supervision and Curriculum Development, St.Louis, Missouri.

Erikson, E. (1963). *Childhood and society (rev. ed.)* New York: Norton.

Gardner, H. (1983). *Frames of mind: The theory of multiple intelligences.* New York: Basic Books.

George, P. S. (1993). Tracking and ability grouping in the middle school: Ten tentative truths. *Middle School Journal, 24* (4), 17-24.

George, P. S., Stevenson, C., Thomason, J., & Beane, J. (1992). *The middle school and beyond.* Alexandria, VA.: Association for Supervision and Curriculum Development.

Glasser, W. (1969). *Schools without failure.* New York: Harper and Row.

Glasser, W. (1984). *Control theory: A new explanation of how we control our lives.* New York: Harper and Row.

Glasser, W. (1990). *The quality school.* New York: HarperCollins Publishers, Inc.

Goodlad, J. (1984). *A place called school: Prospects for the future.* New York: McGraw-Hill Book Company.

Goodrich, H. (1996). Understanding rubrics. *Educational Leadership, 54* (3), 14-17.

Higgins, K. M. & Heglie-King, M. A. (1997). Giving voice to middle school students through portfolio assessment: A journey to mathematical power. *Middle School Journal, 29* (1), 22-29.

Jensen, E. (1998). *Teaching with the brain in mind.* Alexandria, VA: Association for Supervision and Curriculum Development.

Johnston, J. H. (1992). Climate and culture as mediators of school values. In J.L. Irvin (Ed.), *Transforming middle level education: Perspectives and possibilities* (pp. 77-92). Boston: Allyn and Bacon.

Johnston, J. H. (1994). Success for all students. Presentation at Columbia Public Schools, Columbia, MO.

Johnston, J. H., & Markle, G. C. (1986). *What research says to the middle level practitioner.* Columbus, Ohio: National Middle School Association.

Keller, B. M. (1995). Accelerated schools: Hands-on learning in a unified community. *Educational Leadership, 52* (5), 10-13).

Kohn, A. (1991). Caring kids: The role of the schools. *Phi Delta Kappan, 72* (7), 492-506.

Kohn, A. (1993). *Punished by rewards: The trouble with gold stars, incentive plans, A's, praise, and other bribes.* New York: Houghton Mifflin and Co.

Kohn, A. (1994). Grading: The issue is not how but why. *Educational Leadership, 52* (2), 38-41.

Kohn, A. (1996). *Beyond discipline: From compliance to community.* Alexandria, VA: ASCD.

Kramer, L. R. (1992). Young adolescents' perceptions of school. In J. L. Irvin (Ed.), *Transforming middle level education: Perspectives and possibilities* (pp. 28-45). Boston: Allyn and Bacon.

Kreisberg, S. (1992). *Transforming power: Domination, empowerment, and education.* Albany, NY: State University of New York Press.

Landfried, S. E. (1989). "Enabling" undermines responsibility in students. *Educational Leadership, 47* (3), 79-84.

Levine, S., & Coe, C. (1989). Endocrine regulation. In S. Cheren, Ed.), *Psychosomatic Medicine* (pp. 342-344). Madison, CT: International Universities Press, Inc.

Manning, M. L. (1993). *Developmentally appropriate middle schools.* Wheaton, MD: Association for Childhood Education International.

Martino, L. R. (1993). A goal-setting model for young adolescent at risk students. *Middle School Journal, 24* (5), 19-22.

Milgram, J. I. (1985). The development of young adolescents. In J. H. Johnston and J. H. Lounsbury (Eds.), *How fares the ninth grade?* (pp. 5-9). Reston, Virginia: National Association of Secondary School Principals.

Newmann, F. M. (1981). Reducing student alienation in high schools: Implications of theory. *Harvard Educational Review, 51* (4), 546-564.

O'Neil, J. (1990, September). New curriculum agenda emerges for '90s. *Association for Supervision and Curriculum Development Curriculum Update.*

Oakes, J. (1985). *Keeping track: How schools structure inequality.* New Haven: Yale University Press.

O'Neil, J. (1993). Can separate be equal? *Association for Supervision and Curriculum Development Curriculum Update,* June 1993.

88   ACADEMIC SUCCESS THROUGH EMPOWERING STUDENTS

Piaget, J. (1954). *The construction of reality in the child.* New York: Basic Books.

Piaget, J. (1970). *Science of education and the psychology of the child.* New York: Orion Press.

Pool, C. (1997). Maximizing learning: A conversation with Renate Nummela Caine. *Educational Leadership. 54* (6), 11-15.

Purkey, W. W., & Stanley, P. H. (1991). *Invitational teaching, learning, and living.* Washington, DC: National Education Association.

Raebeck, B. (1992). *Transforming middle schools: A guide to whole-school change.* Lancaster, PA: Technomic Publishing Company.

Rogers, C. (1969). *Freedom to learn.* Columbus, Ohio: Charles E. Merrill Publishing Co.

Rogers, C., & Freiberg, H. J. (1994). *Freedom to learn.* New York: MacMillan College Publishing Company.

Ruff, T. P. (1993). Middle school students at risk: What do we do with the most vulnerable children in American education? *Middle School Journal, 24* (5), 10-12.

Scales, P.C. (1991). *A portrait of young adolescents in the 1990s.* Carrboro, NC: Center for Early Adolescence.

Scott, J. E. (1994). Literature circles in the middle school classroom: Developing reading, responding, and responsibility. *Middle School Journal, 26* (2), 37-41.

Sizer, T. (1992). *Nine common principles.* Providence, RI: The Coalition of Essential Schools, Brown University.

Shor, I. (1992). *Empowering education.* Chicago: University of Chicago Press.

Slavin, R. (1990). Achievement effects of ability grouping in secondary schools: A best-evidence synthesis. *Review of Educational Research, 60,* 471-499.

Slavin, R. (1997). Can education reduce social inequity? *Educational Leadership, 55* (4), 6-11.

Spady, W. G., & Marshall, K. J. (1991). Beyond traditional outcome-based education. *Educational Leadership, 49* (2), 67-72.

Strahan, D. (1989). Disconnected and disruptive students: Who they are, why they behave as they do, and what we can do about it. *Middle School Journal, 21* (2), 1-5.

Strahan, D. (1994). Putting middle level perspectives into practice: Creating school cultures that promote caring. *Midpoints, 4* (1).

Sylwester, R. (1995). *A celebration of neurons: An educator's guide to the human brain.* Alexandria, VA: Association for Supervision and Curriculum Development.

Taylor, R., & Reeves, J. (1993). More is better: Raising expectations for students at risk. *Middle School Journal, 24* (5), 13-18.

Thomason, J., & Thompson, M. (1992). Motivation: Moving, learning, mastering, and sharing. In J.L. Irvin (Ed.), *Transforming middle level education: Perspectives and possibilities* (pp. 275-294). Boston: Allyn and Bacon.

Turner, J. C., & Meyer, D. K. (1995). Motivating students to learn: Lessons from a fifth grade math class. *Middle School Journal, 27* (1), 18-25.

Van Hoose, J., & Strahan, D. (1988). *Young adolescent practices: Promoting harmony.* Columbus, Ohio: National Middle School Association.

Vars, G. F. (1997). Student concerns and standards too. *Middle School Journal 28* (4), 44-49.

Vatterott, C. (1990). How middle school climate affects student achievement. *The Transescent, 14* (4), 41-43.

Vatterott, C. (1991). Assessing school climate in the middle level school. *Schools in the Middle: Theory into Practice, April.* Reston, Virginia: National Association of Secondary School Principals.

Vatterott, C. (1995). Student-focused instruction: Balancing limits with freedom in the middle grades. *Middle School Journal, 27* (2), 28-38.

Wasserstein, P. (1995). What middle schoolers say about their schoolwork. *Educational Leadership, 53* (1), 41-43.

Waxman, H. C., Huang, S. L., & Padron, Y. N. (1995). Investigating the pedagogy of poverty in inner-city middle level schools. *Research in Middle Level Education, 18* (2), 1-22.

Wehlage, G., Rutter, R. A., Smith, G. A., Lesko, N., & Fernandez, R. R. (1989). *Reducing the risk: Schools as communities of support.* New York: Falmer Press.

Wheelock, A., & Dorman, G. (1988). *Before it's too late: Dropout prevention in the middle grades.* Available from Search Institute, Minneapolis, MN.

Willis, S. (Ed.) (1993, June) Can separate be equal? *ASCD Curriculum Update.*

NATIONAL MIDDLE SCHOOL ASSOCIATION

National Middle School Association, established in 1973, is the voice for professionals and others interested in the education and well-being of young adolescents. The association has grown rapidly and enrolls members in all fifty states, the Canadian provinces, and forty-two other nations. In addition, fifty-six state, regional, and provincial middle school associations are official affiliates of NMSA.

NMSA is the only association dedicated exclusively to the education, development, and growth of young adolescents. Membership is open to all. While middle level teachers and administrators make up the bulk of the membership, central office personnel, college and university faculty, state department officials, other professionals, parents, and lay citizens are members and active in supporting our single mission – improving the educational experiences of 10-15 year olds. This open and diverse membership is a particular strength of NMSA.

The association publishes *Middle School Journal*, the movement's premier professional journal; *Research in Middle Level Education Quarterly*; *Middle Ground, the Magazine of Middle Level Education; Target*, the association's newsletter; *The Family Connection*, a newsletter for families; *Classroom Connections,* a practical quarterly resource; and a series of research summaries.

The association is also a leading publisher of professional books and monographs in the field of middle level education. Titles provide resources both for understanding and advancing various aspects of the middle school concept and for assisting classroom teachers in planning for instruction. More than seventy NMSA publications are available through the resource catalog as well as selected titles published by other organizations.

The association's highly acclaimed annual conference, which has drawn approximately 10,000 registrants in recent years, is held in the fall. NMSA also sponsors an annual urban education conference and a number of weekend workshops and institutes.

For information about NMSA and its many services contact the Headquarters at 4151 Executive Parkway, Suite 300, Westerville, Ohio, 43081. TELEPHONE: 800-528-NMSA; FAX: 614-895-4750; WEB: WWW. NMSA.ORG.

DATE DUE

FEB 2 6 2002			